MW01600859

SPAIN TRAVEL GUIDE

Your Local Expert Guide to Experience All That Spain Has to Offer | With Easy-to-Follow Itineraries, Top Sights, Hidden Gems, and Budget-Friendly Tips

Carlos Navarro Solera

TABLE OF CONTENTS

The Aims & Objectives of This Book

Whether your trip is your first time or returning, our travel guide is intended to assist anybody wishing to see Spain. The book is meant to provide you with practical advice, cultural insights, and essential knowledge to improve your trips.

- Discover Spain's many provinces, which range from energetic metropolis to historic villages, tranquil countryside to breathtaking coasts.
- Share well-known landmarks and hidden treasures like the Alhambra, Sagrada Família, and Prado Museum as well as less-known locations that highlight Spain's actual appeal.
- Encourage participation in the local culture by means of regional festivals, sampling traditional cuisine, and investigation of handcrafted goods.
- Travel Advice for Spain: To assist you have a seamless and enjoyable vacation, here are some main ideas for getting around, lodging, dining, and knowledge of local traditions.
- By offering useful knowledge and recommendations, help people appreciate Spain's rich heritage, many traditions, and vibrant communities.
- This book will assist you to design a fascinating and original journey around Spain. You will find inspiration here regardless of your interests—art, architecture, history, cuisine, or simply leisurely exploration.

Who Should Read This Book?

Anyone who want to go to Spain and explore the many experiences it offers might find this book interesting. There is something for everyone here regardless of your first experience—that of a seasoned visitor or simply considering a trip to Spain.

- If you appreciate discovering new locations, this book provides vital information on Spain's best attractions and less-known gems.

- Discover various cultural advice and insights if you want to understand more about Spain's fascinating history, vibrant customs, and diverse regional cultures.

- Food and wine enthusiasts will discover many fantastic restaurants and useful advice for dining if you prefer sampling regional cuisine and well-known wines while on tour.

- Adventure Seekers: If you like outdoor pursuits, this book offers suggestions for water sports, climbing, and other thrilling activities in Spain's stunning landscape.

- Independent Travelers: Should you like to design your own itinerary, you will discover useful information, local recommendations, and ideas to boldly explore Spain.

- For both itineraries and last-minute adventurers: Both meticulous planners and free travelers will find open trip options in this book.

- This book is for you if you like to study while seeing Spain and become inspired.

INTRODUCTION

Spain is a fascinating nation with a vibrant culture, stunning landscape, and great passion of life. Every nook and cranny, from the sun-drenched beaches of the Costa del Sol to the historic cobblestone lanes of Toledo, presents a different narrative just waiting discovered. This book transports you to see Spain's well-known landmarks, hidden treasures, and genuine local experiences—not often available on the regular tourist path.

Spain is well-known for its magnificent architecture, exquisite artwork, and distinctive cultural practices and historical history. Among the many great sites to visit in this vibrant nation are the magnificent Alhambra in Granada, the contemporary City of Arts and Sciences in Valencia, and the vital Camino de Santiago Road.

Spain is not just its heritage and architecture. It is about the vibrant character of its cities, the friendliness of its people, and the great cuisine with which they combine. Whether you are sampling modest meals at a crowded market, dancing at a nearby festival, or lounging with coffee in a sleepy town street, Spain encourages you to savor its vibrant way of life.

This book is your reliable friend, providing professional advice, well-chosen recommendations, and helpful hints to enable you to organize your ideal trip. Spain has something for everyone. Discover the historic alleys of Seville, savor the renowned wines from La Rioja, or admire Gaudí's incredible Barcelona architecture.

CHAPTER 1:

INTRODUCTION TO SPAIN:
A Country of Diversity and Culture

Spain is a wonderful nation with rich history, vibrant culture, diversified landscape, and dynamic people. Spain offers something for every kind of visitor, from those who like Mediterranean beaches, elegant architecture, and excellent cuisine. Spain is a fascinating nation to visit as it offers tranquil countryside where life seems slower as well as vibrant cities rich of art and history. This section presents Spain by considering its history, scenery, culture, and what makes it unique travel destination.

Richness of History and Custom

Thousands of years of history define Spain, molded by several tribes like the Romans, Moors, and Visigoths, all of which have contributed to its distinct culture. Particularly with their still-existing aqueducts, amphitheaters, and bridges, the Romans had a significant impact on Spain. The Moors brought their rich cultural traditions including advances in science, arithmetic, and architecture in the eighth century. One of the many constant reminders of this significant period, the Alhambra in Granada is a stunning example of Moorish architecture.

The character of Spain was shaped in great part by the centuries-long effort by Christian nations to recover the nation from Muslim control known as the Reconquista. Late in the fifteenth century, Spain was one nation governed by Catholic Monarchs Ferdinand and Isabella. Their leadership began Spain's expansion as a global power by war and travel. Supported by the Catholic Monarchs, Christopher Columbus's expedition in 1492 found the Americas and let Spain rise to be a major global force for many years.

The rich heritage of Spain reflects its many areas. With seventeen self-governing territories, each with own language, culture, and traditions, the nation boasts for instance, Catalonia has a strong regional identity and a glorious heritage of independence; Catalan is thus quite common alongside Spanish. With its own unique language, Euskara, the Basque Country in the north bases its culture on practices from before Roman times. Key component of Spain's architectural history, Andalusia in southern Spain exhibits a blend of Moorish and Christian inspirations in its structures.

Spain's architecture and monuments as well as its cuisine, music, and events—all still alive today—show evidence of the historical influences from many eras and locations.

Various Locations & Organic beauty

One most obvious feature of Spain's topography is from sunny beaches along its Mediterranean and Atlantic coastlines to the steep mountains of the Pyrenees and the Sierra Nevada, the nation has an incredible range of topography. Spain has a varied terrain. It has lovely mountains, quiet lakes, arid deserts, and green hills.

Beautiful scenery and mountainous topography abound in the northern portions of Spain, including Galicia and Asturias. Like Ireland, Galicia has a strong Celtic past and is well-known for its lush surroundings. It also has quite a remarkable coast. For those who appreciate the outdoors and environment, Asturias is a fantastic area with its Rocky Mountains and verdant trees. The cold temperature of the region differs from the southern national hot and dry climate.

Comprising the center of Spain, the MESETA, or central plateau, is a vast expanse of level ground. Apart from the coastal areas, this area consists of Madrid, the principal metropolis, and has a drier temperature. The region offers a glimpse of classic Spanish life with its antique houses, little villages, and huge farmland.

Andalusia offers unique and breathtaking beauty to the south. With their snowy summits, the Sierra Nevada mountains provide a breathtaking perspective of the farmland and valleys below. Granada's Alhambra displays the Moorish past of the region, while the hills of Andalusia are well-known for their superb farms producing wines of reputation like those from Jerez.

Spain has a physical diversity enhanced by various islands. These include the Balearic Islands in the Mediterranean Sea and the Canary Islands, close to Africa's northwest coast. While the Balearic Islands—which include Mallorca, Ibiza, and Menorca—are well-known for their beaches, blue seas, and vibrant cultural scenes—the Canary Islands are renowned for their volcanic landscape and mild temperature.

Every place has inherent beauty that offers distinct experiences for guests. The Pyrenees are for hiking; Costa Brava's beaches are for lounging; the Canary

Islands' rocky coastlines are for exploration. Spain is a wonderful area to visit all year as it boasts a range of landscapes. Whether your search is for outdoor pursuits, cultural encounters, or a break from work, it offers something for everyone.

Cultural Heritage: Combining Customary Practices

Spain's cultural diversity, which results from its vast history of several areas and the mix of varied impacts throughout the years, is among the most fascinating aspects about it. Native Iberian ideas are combined in Spanish culture with Roman and Moorish inspiration as well as subsequent influences from Jewish and Christian communities. Spain's cultural diversity is seen in its events, music, dancing, art, and cuisine—all of which vary across different regions.

From the southern region of Spain's Andalusia, flamenco is a vibrant and emotive dance and music form. Among Spain's most famous cultural customs is this one. Combining elements from Romani, Jewish, Moorish, and Christian cultures, flamenco music reflects the rich heritage of the region with energetic rhythms and passionate guitar compositions. Especially in Seville, Jerez de la Frontera, and Granada, Flamenco performances abound in emotion and may be seen in many locations throughout Andalusia.

Famous cuisine from Spain is a major component of their way of life. Taste and ingredients abound in Spanish cuisine; every region has its own special specialties. Fresh vegetables, seafood, olive oil, and herbs abound on the Mediterranean diet. It is quite common around coastlines like Valencia and

Catalonia. Fish is quite prominent in the north, particularly in the Basque Country, and pintxos—small meals like tapas—are a staple of the cuisine there.

Madrid and the rest of Spain's central region is well-known for serving classic dishes such as churros con chocolate (fried dough with thick hot chocolate) and cocido Madrileño, a stew including beans, pork, and vegetables. Known among the greatest in the world, Andalusia provides southern cuisine with JAMÓN IBÉRICO (cured ham) and gazpacho, a chilly tomato soup.

Events from Spain are fundamental component of its cultural legacy. Every year the village of Bunol hosts La Tomatina, one of the most well-known festivities. During this occasion, people engage in a great tomato war. Part of the San Fermín celebration, the Running of the Bulls in Pamplona attracts thousands of visitors annually seeking out the thrilling spectacle. Spain is a terrific destination to explore culture all year long since every region offers unique festivals like the vibrant Feria de Abril in Seville and the entertaining Carnival in Tenerife.

The construction history of Spain is similarly diversified. From Gothic temples and Romanesque cathedrals in the north to Moorish homes and castles in the south, the nation's structures reveal its rich history. Renowned builder Antoni Gaudí designed Barcelona's Sagrada Familia, among the most well-known constructions in Spain. Millions of visitors come annually from its huge structures and thorough designs. Reflecting Spain's blend of many civilizations, two examples of her exquisite architecture are the Roman canal in Segovia and the Alhambra in Granada.

Spain's Current Identity: A Nation Under Development

Though Spain is a nation that is developing and evolving, it has strong cultural values. Spain changed from a dictatorship to a democracy with the death of despot Francisco Franco in 1975, therefore fostering development in culture. By joining the European Union in 1986, the nation's economy grew, and its global connection grew as well. Today Spain combines the ancient with the modern. Modern art and design coexist with traditional events; old structures surround newly constructed ones.

Spain has a diversified economy with significant areas like tourism, agriculture, industry, and technology. Though they retain their rich cultural legacy, the cities across the nation are vibrant hubs of fresh ideas, led in technology by Madrid and Barcelona. Spain is now well-known for its creative industries like design, fashion, and cinema. Many Spanish filmmakers and designers are becoming well-known all over.

Spain is a nation going through political and social transformation. Talks on regional authority and the campaign for Catalonia's independence highlight how dynamically Spain's politics are evolving. With local identities coexisting with a strong national pride, Spain remains unified despite these challenges.

As Spain enters the contemporary era, it is modernizing but still clings to its past and preserves its cultural customs. This blend of history, culture, and modernism offers visitors an intriguing experience in one of Europe's most diverse and vibrant nations. Whether you are visiting its cities, savoring its cuisine, or going to its events, Spain offers a vibrant and unforgettable travel experience.

CHAPTER 2:

HOW TO PLAN YOUR TRIP TO SPAIN:
The Ultimate Guide

Spain has much to offer renowned cuisine, sunny beaches, old cities, and little villages. Whether your journey to Spain is first-time or returning to experience more of its culture, you need carefully arrange your travel. Covering when to travel, how to get around, must-see sites, and advice for handling cultural differences will help you arrange a fantastic vacation to Spain.

Deciding When to See Spain

When you start to arrange your trip to Spain, one of the first decisions you will have to make is on visiting date. Spain's diversified topography results in many climates. What you want to accomplish will determine the ideal time to visit.

With pleasant winters close to the shore and hot, dry summers, Spain has a Mediterranean climate. On the other hand, the national center—especially areas like Madrid—has more severe climate with scorching summers and frigid winters. The temperature runs differently from north to south. Cooler and gentler are northern regions like Galicia and the Basque Country.

Most visitors find the ideal periods to arrive in spring and autumn. From April to June and September to October, Spain has pleasant climate from mild to warm conditions ideal for travel. Less summer traffic in these months allows travel to be more laid down.

If you want to avoid crowds and heat, think about visiting in the winter, from December to February. While certain tourist destinations may shut during the low season, the colder months draw less guests and lower hotel and airline rates. Those who like winter activities can find excellent locations to ski Spain's northern highlands, including the Pyrenees and Sierra Nevada.

Visit Spain in the summer from June to August if you like a joyful and entertaining trip. The hectic Christmas season of the nation will please you. Be ready for the heat, particularly in southern regions like Andalusia where temperatures could reach forty (104°F). This is also when Spain's most well-known celebrations take place—La Tomatina in Bunol and the Running of the Bulls in Pamplona. For those who like large gatherings and wild celebrations, these events provide entertaining cultural encounters.

Discover many regions of Spain.

There are seventeen zones in Spain, each with its distinct customs, language, and culture. Understanding the regional variations can help you to better enjoy your vacation as every town presents a unique perspective of Spanish living.

If you like construction and art, you should most certainly visit Northeastern Catalonia, particularly its metropolis Barcelona. Barcelona is one of the most well-known cities in Spain because of its contemporary architecture, particularly that of Antoni Gaudí, and its gorgeous seashore surroundings. Spoken alongside Spanish, Catalan is the language of Catalonia. This reveals its unique cultural background.

Beautiful structures like the Alhambra and the Mezquita help to depict Spain's Moorish heritage in southern Andalusia's cities include Seville, Granada, and Córdoba. The flamenco music and dance of Andalusia are well-known emotive and passionate works of art vital to the local culture.

If you want more sedate, rural locations, the northern parts of Galicia and Asturias include magnificent towns and landscapes. Though they are not particularly well-liked by visitors, these locations provide a genuine glimpse of old Spanish life. Galicia is well known for its seafood and unique local dialects; Asturias is renowned for its rich culture and gorgeous mountain landscape.

Comprising its own language, Euskara, and distinctive cuisine habits, the northern Basque Country offers a unique experience. Modern architecture of Bilbao is well-known, as is the Guggenheim Museum. Particularly pintxos, little tapas-like cuisine, San Sebastián is well-known for its great food and beautiful beaches.

Finally, Madrid, the major metropolis, provides a central location for national exploration. The city has fine streets, nightlife, and great museums like the Prado and Reina Sofia. Madrid is a fantastic base for your journey as it is simple to go other large cities and regions of Spain.

- Along with stunning structures like the Alhambra in Granada and the Mezquita in Córdoba, Andalusia is well-known for its Moorish culture, flamenco music and dance. See stunning white villages, Costa del Sol's warm beaches, and energetic Seville—known for its historic bullrings and festivals.

- Special culture, language, and architecture—like the well-known Sagrada Família in Barcelona—have come to define Catalonia. Take in the Mediterranean shoreline, Gaudí's architectural masterpieces, and the vibrant Gothic Quarter scene.

- Especially pintxos, Basque Country boasts distinct cuisine, language, and culture. See the Guggenheim Museum in Bilbao, then see coastal areas like San Sebastián, well-known for its cuisine and immaculate beaches.

- Castile and León are a historical region with castles and medieval cities. See Salamanca, a UNESCO city noted for its historic university, and Segovia, which has a Roman canal and stunning Alcazar.

- Galicia has unique Celtic culture, misty shoreline, and verdant surroundings. See Santiago de Compostela, the last point of the well-traveled Camino de Santiago path. Savor good seafood and the distinctive wine from the region, ALBARIÑO.

- Valencia is regarded as the birthplace of paella and has beautiful Mediterranean beaches as well as the City of Arts and Sciences. See the vibrant ancient town of Valencia as well as the surrounding countryside noted for its orange trees and beautiful gardens.

- Madrid is Spain's capital as well as a hub for history, art, and culture. See Retiro Park, the Prado Museum, and the Royal Palace. Also meander through the crowded streets and tapas restaurants in the La Latina and MALASAÑA neighborhoods.

- Mallorca, Ibiza, Menorca, and Formentera together form Balearic Islands. Beautiful beaches, vibrant nightlife—especially on Ibiza—as well as a rich history and culture abound on these islands Discover little cities, historic structures, and mouthwatering Mediterranean cuisine.

- Comprising a chain of islands off Africa's northwest coast, the Canary Islands are well-known for their volcanoes, year-round mild temperature, and stunning beaches. See Gran CANARIA'S sand dunes, Teide National Park in Tenerife, and savor the peace of La Palma.

- Don Quixote was conceived in Castilla-La Mancha, where windmills abound. See the windmills at Consuegra, see the historic town of Toledo, and take in the expansive fields producing Spain's famed wines.

- Murcia has a pleasant climate, excellent agricultural, and beautiful beaches like Mar Menor. See Murcia's lovely antique structures and savor its energetic vibe.

- Little known yet historically significant is Extremadura. It has wonderful sites like Cáceres and Trujillo as well as Roman remains in Mérida. For those who like animals, Extremadura is a fantastic destination with plenty of lovely natural areas under protection.

- Rich in history and with gorgeous Pyrenees mountains ideal for hiking and skiing is Aragon. See old cities like Albarracin and the medieval city of Zaragoza, home of the Basilica del Pilar.

- One little region famed for its farming and winemaking is La Rioja. Taste excellent Rioja wines on a wine tour in picturesque cities like Haro and Logroño, then enjoy the serene countryside.

- Navarre is a diversified region with mountains and plenty of rivers. See Pamplona, well known for the Running of the Bulls, and explore the lovely desert-like BARDENAS Reales region.

- Beautiful beaches, rugged mountains, and verdant farms define Asturias. See the historic city of Oviedo, lovely beaches, and Picos de Europa National Park.

- Cantabria is a beachfront region with great beaches, verdant hills, and the incredible Altamira Caves—which include prehistoric cave drawings. Go to Santander for a mix of seaside leisure and culture.

- Nestled in the Pyrenees, VAL D'ARAN has winter skiing, beautiful villages, and breathtaking mountain vistas. For those who like adventure and the natural world, this is fantastic.

- Apart from Valencia city, explore the beautiful coastline, charming villages like ALBUFERA, and unique areas include the Caves of San José and the old city of CASTELLÓN in the COMUNIDAD Valenciana.

- Madrid Region: See beautiful sites like Alcalá de Henares, the birthplace of Cervantes, and savor walks and animal viewing in the nearby natural surroundings of Madrid.

- Apart from the nightlife, discover the peaceful Ibizan countryside, dotted with modest bays, soft hills, and classic white cottages.

Establishing Your Budget

Although Spain is an affordable European destination, your location and desired kind of experience will affect the pricing. Whether your trip budget is limited, or you are searching for something elegant, Spain offers options for all sorts of visitors, therefore it is crucial to create a budget before your trip.

From affordable hostels and guesthouses to luxurious five-star hotels and elegant spas, Spain has a variety of lodging options. Particularly during peak travel, big cities such as Barcelona, Madrid, and Seville often have higher hotel rates. If you are open to searching beyond the popular tourist destinations, smaller towns and rural locations provide less expensive options to help you remain within your means.

There are plenty of dining choices in Spain to fit various budgets. A terrific way to sample regional cuisine without going broke is with tapas, little bits of food frequently presented with beverages. Various regions have special cuisine; for Valencia, paella; for the Basque Country, pintxos. Usually, dining out in smaller locations is less expensive than in major cities, where fashionable restaurants and international cuisine may push prices higher. Look at local marketplaces if you want to save money. For lunch or dinner at home, you could find fresh fruits, vegetables, meats, cheeses.

Particularly if you make advantage of Spain's excellent public transit system, the nation boasts quite affordable transportation expenditures. In cities like Madrid and Barcelona, public transportation including trains, buses, and the metro is reasonably priced and user-friendly. Linking major cities, the rapid AVE rail system facilitates quick and simple transit between places. If you want to explore rural regions or locations public transportation cannot readily access, you may have to hire a vehicle.

For those on a tight budget, Spain is a perfect location with its cheaper cost of living than many other European nations. Planning your activities ahead of time and knowing additional expenses include museum tickets, gratuities, and transportation can help you to avoid overspending.

Deciding on the Length of Your Trip

Though Spain offers numerous attractions and things to enjoy, how long should you be staying? Your trip's length will depend on your preferred destination, what you like, and the speed of travel desired.

If your visit is the first time, a week-long excursion is a fantastic choice. This schedule allows you to visit large cities such Madrid and Barcelona and arrange a day excursion to a surrounding location. In a week you may see the cities' art, history, and culture, relax on the beach, and taste Spanish cuisine and wine. A typical travel schedule might have you spending two or three days in Madrid, two or three days in Barcelona, and one day excursion to a neighboring location like Toledo or Montserrat.

Two weeks will allow you to see more places and more completely experience Spanish culture. If you have more time, you may tour the northern coast to see places like Bilbao and San Sebastián, visit Andalusia to experience its Moorish heritage, or investigate the wine districts of La Rioja. This time lets you enjoy more sports, side excursions, and cultural events while also traveling more readily across the nation.

You have numerous choices for things to do if you have one month or more to spend in Spain. Important cities, breathtaking landscapes, outdoor activities in the Pyrenees or along the Mediterranean coast, and the laid-back Spanish way of life are just waiting for you to discover. Longer trips allow you to travel more leisurely and take in the nation's varied landscapes and local cultures.

Booking Your Flights and Places to Stay: Strategies

Booking your flights and lodging comes next after you decide when and where to go. With significant international centers in Madrid, Barcelona, Seville, and Valencia, Spain has strong ties to the globe. Early airline booking is crucial as, particularly during busy travel seasons, costs may rise as the departure date approaches.

Spain has several lodging options to suit varying budgets and tastes. Small hotels, hostels, and luxury spas abound in towns for lodging choices. Away from the cities, in rural areas and seaside districts, you may discover friendly guesthouses, traditional inns, and farm stays allowing you a closer view of life in Spain.

Booking your stay ahead of time is a smart concept, particularly if you want to visit crowded tourist destinations such as Barcelona, Madrid, or Seville during their peak seasons. Consider purchasing a vacation house or apartment if you want more genuine experience. This will establish a closer relationship with the local environment and enable you to feel more engaged in the surroundings.

Preparing oneself for Spanish customs and manners.

Although Spain is a welcoming nation, knowing its traditions and way of life can help you to have an enjoyable and civil travel. Generally speaking, Spaniards see time more relaxed than people from other nations. Therefore, particularly in the south, do not be surprised if businesses or restaurants open later in the day. Some areas still have siesta afternoon breaks when individuals pause for a few hours in various companies.

Spanish people like their cuisine, hence dining together is really important in their daily life. Say "buenos días" (good morning) or "BUENAS TARDES" (good afternoon) to the server when you go out to lunch. Though not obligatory, normally approximately 5–10% of the bill is tipped.

Besides, Spain is renowned for its social scene. An integral component of society is eating and drinking together with friends and family. Locals may frequently be seen eating leisurely, laid-back dinners late into the evening. Slower living may improve your vacation and enable you to meet Spanish people.

Making a travel to Spain is an interesting vacation requiring proper planning. Choose the correct time to come, read about its many areas, create a realistic budget, and really engage yourself in the local culture to make your vacation to Spain pleasant and unforgettable. From its heritage and gorgeous landscape to its mouthwatering cuisine, Spain has much to offer. Your visit might be remarkable with some preparation.

CHAPTER 3:

HIDDEN GEMS:
Exploring Spain's Best-Kept Secrets

Spain has a rich heritage, vibrant culture, and breathtaking landscape. Although cities like Barcelona, Madrid, and Seville are well-liked travel destinations, Spain also has numerous less-known gems just waiting for discovery. These less-known locations help guests discover hidden treasures outside of the typical tourist destinations and provide a unique perspective of Spain's rich culture and stunning scenery. Quiet mountain communities in Spain, gorgeous seaside towns, and historic monuments that will astound visitors abound. This section will introduce you to some of the most fascinating and under-known locations in Spain you should most certainly visit.

The Beautiful Town of Ronda

Many people overlook the lovely town of Ronda in Andalusia. Set high in the mountains, just on the brink of a deep valley, Ronda offers breathtaking views of the surroundings. The Puente Nuevo (New Bridge) traverses the canyon and connects both sides of this town, therefore defining its unique position. The bridge offers one of the most breathtaking vistas in Spain, hence it is ideal to enjoy the blend of Moorish and Spanish architecture there.

Apart from its well-known bridge, Ronda has a rich heritage spanning Roman times. One of Spain's oldest bullrings, the Plaza de Toros in the town allows visitors to investigate the long-standing bullfighting practices of the nation. The village is a perfect place to unwind and savor life at a slower pace because its little stone lanes lead to beautiful parks, white homes, and serene gardens. Ronda provides a unique experience away from the crowded tourist areas in Andalusia's larger cities, whether you are savoring the view from the bridge or strolling in the ancient town.

- Renowned Puente Nuevo (New Bridge) by Ronda spans the El Tajo canyon and offers breathtaking views of the historic town below and the countryside.

- Ronda's historical significance began with the Romans and grew with the Moors. Old buildings, cobblestone streets, and well-kept sculptures all reflect their long history.

- One of the first and most well-known bullrings in Spain is the Plaza de Toros, Ronda's Bullring Anyone fascinated in the background of bullfighting has to visit it. It has a museum concentrating on the technique as well.

- Discover the historic town of Ronda, where you may meander down little lanes, see white homes, visit local businesses, and relax in beautiful squares including cafés.

- Discover the well-kept Arab baths from the 13th century located at the base of the gorge. They highlight Ronda's Moorish origins and superb technology.

- Visit Mirador de Althaea and Mirador de Ronda for breathtaking views of the lovely mountains and river that will astound your breathlessness.

- Ronda is situated 120 meters above the El Tajo Gorge. Many walking pathways leading to the gorge's bridge provide breathtaking views of the town and area.

- Visit the 14th-century Moorish Mondragón mansion and the Church of Santa María la Mayor, which was constructed where a mosque had stood. These sites exhibit Ronda's numerous architecture types.

- Ronda is known for its wines and is in the Sierra de Ronda wine region. Take a wine tour where you may sample regional wines and take in the lovely views of the surrounding countryside.

- From geology to vintage musical instruments, Ronda boasts the fascinating Museo Lara where one may see several exhibitions. It helps one to grasp the cultural history of the place.

- Saunter about the gorgeous Alameda del Tajo gardens, next to the canyon, in privacy. These parks provide good locations for sitting to take in the surroundings' sights.

- Day visits from places like Málaga, Seville, and Marbella are well-known in Ronda. Its peaceful atmosphere makes it a fantastic place to spend the night as well.

- Conventional Andalusian Cooking: In one of Ronda's classic restaurants or tapas bars, sample local cuisine such "RABO DE TORO," (oxtail stew), "JAMÓN SERRANO," and "TARTA DE ALMENDRA," (almond cake).

- Particularly with sunset views from the bridge, Ronda's gorgeous surroundings, old streets, and pleasant mood make it the perfect place for a romantic getaway.

- Finding the Nearby Rural Area: Perfect for climbing, nature hikes, and appreciating the breathtaking vistas of Ronda's rugged hills and valleys is the Sierra de las Nieves Natural Park all around.

- Ronda organizes cultural events: Participate in customary activities highlighting the town's rich traditions like the Feria de Pedro Romero, a bullfighting fair, and Semana Santa, the Holy Week festivities.

- Perfect for Photographers: Ronda's gorgeous bridges, historic buildings, and breathtaking landscape highlighting Andalusia's splendor will appeal to photographers.

- Little Shops and Cafes: Rest in a café with a coffee or local wine, then spend a leisurely day shopping for local crafts, ceramics, and leather goods, or just staring over the canyon.

- Starting with your visits to neighboring towns, such SETENIL de las Bodegas, famed for its cave dwellings, and GRAZALEMA, which is well-known for its white villages and parks, Ronda is a fantastic site to start your day adventures.

- Ronda is a terrific spot for anybody searching for a peaceful escape loaded with history, nature, and beauty because it offers a serene alternative to the crowded cities of southern Spain.

The Curious CUEVA DE LA PILETA

An important historical landmark, the CUEVA DE LA PILETA is an ancient cave in Málaga, Spain. This cave, deep in the highlands, has more than 20,000-year-old ancient rock art. The images of people and animals in the drawings provide us with a fascinating window into the life of early humans in the vicinity. The cave is less well-known, so it is more intriguing and enigmatic.

Compared to the packed throng at Spain's most famous sites, visiting CUEVA DE LA PILETA provides a peaceful experience and seems like going back in time. Underlining its history, the cave provides guided excursions via narrow pathways highlighting stunning rock art. This unique site allows you to interact with Spain's ancient legacy if you find interest in its prehistoric past.

The Costa Brava Quiet Beaches

Though the Costa Brava in northern Catalonia is one of Spain's best-kept secrets, the country is renowned for its beautiful Mediterranean shoreline. Though well-known locations like Barcelona and Valencia attract a lot of interest, the Costa Brava offers a more subdued and natural experience. Large numbers of visitors have not had much of an impact on this rocky coastline, which has secluded bays, glistening clean seas, and beautiful fishing villages.

Nestled between cliffs and pine trees, Costa Brava has a combination of gently sandy beaches and secret rocky areas. Among the loveliest beaches in the region are PLATJA de Castell, a peaceful beach with golden sands ideal for swimming and tanning, and CALA MONTJOI, a secret cove with turquoise seas. Usually less crowded than the public beaches, these hidden ones are ideal for leisure and discovery.

Apart from its beaches, Costa Brava has other lovely communities worth visiting. White homes, lovely cobblestone walkways, and breathtaking views of the sea define towns such CADAQUÉS and TOSSA DE MAR. Excellent hiking paths near the seaside in the region provide breathtaking views of the Mediterranean and access to some of Spain's most pictures-perfect locations.

The Perfect Town of CUDILLO

Many visitors ignore the vibrant fishing village of CUDILLERO, in the northern Spain region of Asturias. Charming CUDILLERO is in a lovely valley with views of the rocky shore. Its vibrantly colored homes perched on the high slopes are well-known. The town seems like you are in a painting with its unique structures and lovely perspective.

Especially its daily fresh fish catch, CUDILLERO is well-known for its seafood. Fresh local fish, prawns, and squid dishes created by the village's restaurants and taverns provide some of the greatest seafood available in Spain. The dock of the village, dotted with vintage fishing boats, seems very authentic. Along the coast or to the overlook, visitors may leisurely walk to enjoy stunning views of the sea and hamlet.

Beautiful but not well-known to international visitors, CUDILLERO is a fantastic place for everyone wishing to savor actual Spanish beach life. It is a unique location in northern Spain because of its tranquilly, breathtaking vistas, and good cuisine.

BARDENAS Reales: Uncovering Hidden Beauty

Large semi-desert in southern Navarre, Spain, the BARDENAS Reales is located. Its landscape is distinctive from that of other parts of the nation. With amazing rock forms, steep valleys, and vast stretches of dry, cracked earth, this UNESCO Biosphere Reserve has an arid terrain. Though odd, the BARDENAS Reales offers a unique habitat with Mediterranean tortoises, wild boars, and birds of prey.

With climbing, motorcycling, and off-road driving among other activities, the BARDENAS Reales is ideal for nature lovers and explorers. With various paths leading visitors over the desert level and past some breathtaking rock formations, the region is ideal for strolling or bicycling. With ancient Roman remains scattered across the area and old caverns discovered all around, the BARDENAS Reales has a rich history. This is a fantastic place to enjoy a quiet and unique environment and get away from daily life.

The Middle Ages Village of ALBARRACÍN

Small historical hamlet ALBARRACÍN is located in Teruel province, Aragón region. There is a good reason this little-known gem is often regarded as one of the most beautiful cities in Spain. ALBARRACÍN has a lovely, timeless vibe from its well-kept historic buildings, small, winding lanes, and dirt trails. Situated on a hill, the town offers breathtaking views of the surroundings covered in dense forests and sharp rocks.

Navigating ALBARRACÍN is like returning to the Middle Ages. Among the various fantastic historical buildings in the area are the Church of El Salvador and the ALBARRACÍN Castle from the eleventh century. Both sites provide excellent views of the town and the surrounding agricultural area. Renowned for their pink and yellow painted historic homes, ALBARRACÍN makes the community appealing and welcoming for visitors.

Though it is lovely, ALBARRACÍON receives less tourism than other Spanish old cities. For those who want to appreciate Spain's history and beauty free from the throngs, this is the perfect spot. Perfect for a leisure getaway, ALBARRACÍN offers a peaceful haven among Spain's lovely countryside.

The stunning ORDESA and Monte Perdido National Park

One of Spain's most beautiful natural locations, ORDESA and Monte Perdido National Park is situated in the Pyrenees Mountains for those who like the natural world, this UNESCO World Heritage site—which has breathtaking cliffs, deep valleys, waterfalls, and clean rivers—is heaven. Among the many species found in the park are golden eagles, marmots, and ibex.

Walkers love the park as it provides several paths ranging from short walks to challenging multi-day excursions. The most well-known path, the ORDESA Valley trek provides visitors with breathtaking scenery featuring the renowned Cola de Caballo waterfall. Among the highest summits in the Pyrenees, Monte Perdido peaks 3,355 meters (10,975 feet—is included in the park. ORDESA and Monte Perdido National Park is a fantastic place offering great beauty and chances for outdoor activities if you are seeking thrills and breathtaking vistas.

The calm village of Sos del Rey CATÓLICO

Beautiful historic town with fascinating heritage is Sos del Rey CATÓLICO in Zaragoza province. King Ferdinand II of Aragon is famously from the hamlet. His marriage to Castilian Isabella united Spain in the fifteenth century. Mass tourism has not harmed the significant historical site Sos, which lets guests have a real and peaceful experience of rural Spain.

Little lanes dotted with historic old structures, such as the Church of San Esteban and the Castillo de Sos, a fortress offering fantastic views of the surroundings, abound throughout the settlement. Particularly dishes like TERNASCO (roast lamb) and JAMÓN DE TERUEL (cured ham), the area is well-known for its mouthwatering native cuisine. Away from the crowded tourist attractions, SOS DEL REY CATÓLICO allows visitors appreciate Spain's rich heritage in a calm and picturesque location.

Spain has numerous hidden beauties; the sites included in this chapter are just a few of the many waiting to be explored. Spain offers numerous hidden gems just waiting for you to discover whether your search is for natural beauty, history, or true cultural experiences. Discovering less-known parts of the nation can help you find a side of Spain often missed by visitors. Anyone who wishes to explore a different side of Spain, away from the regular tourist sites, will find these hidden treasures fantastic. They provide a more real, intimate, and memorable experience of this beautiful and diverse nation.

CHAPTER 4:

MADRID:
The Heart of Spain – Flamenco, Fútbol, and Tapas

Madrid, Spain's capital, is a vibrant metropolis that captures the vitality, feeling, and range of the nation overall. Madrid is the political and commercial hub of Spain and is in the middle of the nation. It is also a site bursting with pleasure, history, and culture. Madrid brings together a blend of historic beauty and contemporary life with its outstanding museums, elegant architecture, crowded squares, and energetic streets. Key components of Spanish culture, flamenco dance, soccer, and tapas—which define Madrid— are available for visitors to the city to experience. This section will teach you how to see Madrid like a native and assist you to grasp its core.

Flamenco: Spain's Heart

Spanish culture revolves around flamenco; hence Madrid is one of the ideal venues to appreciate this vibrant art. Though people all throughout the nation have embraced and modified the dance and singing form known as flamenco, which originated in southern Spain's Andalusian region Key components of Spain's culture include Flamenco's powerful rhythms, passionate guitar music, moving singing, and energetic dancing; Madrid is the ideal venue to experience these feelings of this art.

Flamenco originated in Andalusia, but Madrid has grown to be a significant venue for performance. With seasoned performers and fresh artists presenting thrilling events, the city has some of the top flamenco venues in Spain. Popular in Madrid, the renowned Corral de la MORERÍA hosts flamenco performances. Live flamenco shows in a small space will let visitors experience a remarkable evening. Many well-known flamenco performers have performed here, and its presentations highlight the great emotions, passion, and skill that define flamenco.

Flamenco is a means of expression for intense emotions not just a performance. Strong emotions like love, grief, and desire are shown in the dance via its energetic dancing and expressive arm motions. Often reflecting on life, hardships, and love, singing, or CANTE, narrates tales. By producing intricate rhythms and melodies that captivate the audience into the performance, the guitar—or toque—helps to complement the song. From little venues to large stages, flamenco events abound in Madrid for you to enjoy. It is a wonderful approach to value Spain's culture.

Football: Deep Love for Sport

Without including sports, which define Madrid's identity, no discussion about the city would be whole. Real Madrid and Atlético Madrid are Madrid's two of the most well-known and outstanding football teams worldwide. Strong FÚTBOL enthusiasts, Madrileños are clearly passionate about the game all across the city. The yells at neighborhood pubs and the packed Santiago Bernabéu Stadium highlight exactly how vibrant and dynamic Madrid's soccer scene is.

Renowned and successful soccer team Real Madrid resides in Madrid. Soccer enthusiasts from all across the globe frequent their hometown, Santiago Bernabéu, which is quite popular. Among the greatest football players ever, including Cristiano Ronaldo, Zinedine Zidane, and Alfredo Di Stéfano, the stadium has towering seats and an intense atmosphere. Attending a game at the Santiago Bernabéu is remarkable. An amazing environment is created by the loud applause from the audience, fast games, and excitement of seeing elite players in action.

Conversely, Atlético Madrid, the second elite club in the capital, offers a different but nonetheless very fascinating FÚTBOL experience. Atlético Madrid features committed players and a disciplined, industrious approach to play. Designed for Atlético's committed supporters, Wanda Metropolitano is a new stadium. One of the most thrilling games in the history of soccer, Real Madrid, and Atlético Madrid's heated rivalry—known as the Madrid Derby—has extraordinary intensity. Madrid offers an incredible experience that will wow any sports enthusiast, regardless of your passion—one of the Madrid teams or just adore football.

Madrid nevertheless has a vibrant FÚTBOL culture in its packed sports pubs and neighborhood venues even if you cannot see a live match. On game days, pubs fill with residents and visitors drawn together to support their preferred team. The happiness and vitality in these locations highlight the significance of FÚTBOL for Madrid's character.

Tapas: An Eating Custom

Madrid's cuisine is among the nicest things about it; specifically, tapas, a staple of Spanish cuisine, is very outstanding. Usually presented with beverages, tapas are little yet delicious meals that are incredibly significant in Madrid social life. Small food dishes called tapas originated in Andalusia, where they were stacked atop wine glasses to ward off flies. Tapas are now a mainstay of Spanish cuisine, and Madrid has some of the greatest ones anywhere.

In Madrid, tapas are about having fun rather than just cuisine. One enjoyable way to get together with friends and relatives is to savor wonderful food, conversation, and beverages is for tapas. The atmosphere at Madrid's tapas bars is relaxed and welcoming; most of them provide good cuisine designed for sharing. Tapas abound in Madrid, ranging from pickled olives, calamari, and Spanish omelet (tortilla Española) to flavorful cured ham (JAMON IBÉRICO), spicy sausage (chorizo).

The historic sections of La Latina, MALASAÑA, and the Mercado de San Miguel include some of Madrid's top tapas locations. From one tapas bar to another, residents and visitors travel from one busy bar scene eating various meals and appreciating the vibrant city environment. La Latina allows you to stroll through little lanes lined with antique pubs. Many of them are classic Spanish fare such patatas bravas (fried potatoes topped with spicy tomato sauce) and croquetas, deep-fried balls stuffed with cheese, ham, or chicken. Near Plaza Mayor, the lively Mercado de San Miguel is a food market where visitors may savor a range of mouthwatering delicacies like fresh seafood and unique cheeses.

Usually presented as appetizers or snacks, tapas may also be used to create a full meal. Typical tapas evenings in Madrid could start with some light appetizers and then include heavier dishes like grilled meat, seafood paella, or a full stew called COCIDO MADRILEÑO, which calls for beans, pork, and vegetables. Usually paired with local wines such as the well-known Rioja or a refreshing drink called TINTO DE VERANO, a wine cocktail that is quite popular in the summer, tapas are savored.

Tapas reflect Madrid's vibrant and shared culture rather than just cuisine. A major everyday activity in the city, going out for tapas is a fantastic opportunity to really enjoy the Spanish way of life. Whether you are in a small bar with a bottle of wine or savoring grilled veggies with friends, tapas reflect the pleasure of life, the importance of community, and the appreciation of good, basic food.

Madrid's Curious History and Contemporary Culture

Though the city's heritage and culture are much richer than just these three items, flamenco, soccer, and tapas are well-known elements of Madrid. Madrid has evolved throughout the years quite a bit. Originally a Moorish outpost, it evolved in the sixteenth century to be Spain's capital. Retiro Park, the Prado Museum, and the Royal Palace, among other significant cultural sites, highlight the city's rich past.

Madrid embraces modern living and has elegant structures, contemporary art galleries, and vibrant nightlife capable of rivaling that of other large European cities. Among the most often used streets in Madrid is the Gran Vía. It is ideal to savor the vibrant culture of the city as it is loaded with theaters, movies, stores, and restaurants. Among the best art and cultural events in Spain are found in Madrid. Among the noteworthy events are the San Isidro Festival, which commemorates the patron saint of the city with parades, music, and dancing, Madrid Fashion Week, and Madrid International Film Festival.

Madrid has a strong feeling of community and local pride even if it is large and has a varied environment. MADRILEÑOS, the inhabitants of Madrid, are kind and inviting. Their city's unique traditions and culture make them proud. Madrid's energetic character will be seen by visitors in its busy cafés, bars, large streets, and old neighborhoods.

- Madrid's history starts with the Moors erecting a fortification in the ninth century. King Philip II named it the capital of Spain in 1561, therefore affecting the political and cultural relevance of the city in that nation.

- Madrid has the neighboring Almudena Cathedral as well as the Royal Palace, the largest royal residence in Europe. These both are significant markers of the ancient royal history of the city.

- Particularly in the prominent Plaza Mayor and the exquisite buildings in the Habsburg neighborhood, which combine Renaissance and Baroque forms, the Habsburg dynasty affected the architecture of the city.

- For Madrid, the Spanish Civil War, which took place 1936 to 1939, was quite significant. The battle emotionally changed the residents of the city and left long-lasting harm to it. See significant sites from this era, including the Valley of the Fallen.

- Madrid has a rich artistic legacy with contemporary art housed at the Reina Sofía Museum and well-known pieces found in the Prado Museum. Important pieces of Goya, Velázquez, Picasso, and Dalí paintings highlight Madrid's value of culture.

- Literary Tradition: Madrid has been a major hub for both modern Spanish writers and Golden Age authors like Cervantes. The Cervantes Institute and the Literary Quarter are only two locations honoring the great literary legacy of the city.

- Modern Madrid first emerged in the 19th century as the city expanded with the construction of expansive avenues like Gran Vía and bettering infrastructure. Neighborhoods like Salamanca and CHAMBERÍ clearly exhibit a shift to neoclassical and varied designs.

- Famous historical venues where government events, parades, and daily activities take place include Madrid's principal squares, Puerta del Sol, Plaza Mayor, and Plaza de CIBELES.

- Madrid, continually evolving with new theaters, art galleries, and contemporary art venues—especially in places like MALASAÑA and CHUECA—is the cultural hub of Spain.

- Madrid's culinary culture blends traditional Spanish cuisine with fresh, contemporary ideas in gastronomic evolution. Try unique dining experiences at contemporary food markets like Mercado de San Miguel and savor classic tapas such "patatas bravas."

- Madrid is well-known for its vibrant nightlife, which has tapas cafés, classic flamenco performances, chic rooftop pubs and nightclubs. This image captures the friendly and entertaining atmosphere of the city.

- contemporary Architecture: The city's skyline features an original mix of contemporary architecture, including the innovative structures in the MATADERO Madrid cultural center and the futuristic towers in the Cuatro Torres Business Area.

- Retiro Park and Casa de Campo in Madrid are among the green spaces there where one may unwind apart from the hectic metropolis. Walking and outdoor enjoyment abound in Retiro Park, which has art galleries and a fishing lake.

- Every year Madrid has several celebrations of its contemporary and traditional traditions. Among them are the energetic San Isidro Festival, the vivid Madrid Pride, and the varied Madrid Fashion Week.

- Madrid's districts reflect the range of the city's culture. La Latina has a bohemian vibe; Salamanca is costly and sophisticated; CHUECA welcomes the LGBTQ+ population. Every region has unique combinations of history, architecture, and culture.

- Part of Madrid's culture is flamenco music and dance, quite significant. See the present music culture of the city with pop, rock, and dance forms; enjoy events at historical sites like Corral de la MORERÍA.

- Shopping in Madrid is fantastic. From elegant businesses on Calle de Serrano to vibrant street markets like El RASTRO, where you may purchase antiques, clothing, and handcrafted goods, you will find everything.

- Modern street art is gaining favor in Madrid, particularly in areas like LAVAPIÉS and MALASAÑA. Paintings and installations here provide the city with vitality and inventiveness.

- Madrid has well-known cultural celebrations such the Madrid Book Fair and the Madrid International Film Festival, where local talent from all across the globe highlights their works.

- The city exhibits a combination of contemporary and historic construction. This is seen in the historic Royal Palace beside contemporary vertical parks like the CAIXAFORUM.

- Madrid is known for its progressive and friendly culture, which reflects in its acceptance of all kinds of individuals, support of equal rights for all genders, and strong fighting for LGBTQ+ rights.

Combining history and modernism, Madrid is a city that fairly captures Spain. Through the passion of flamenco music, the thrill of soccer (FÚTBOL), and the mouthwatering flavor of tapas Madrid provides visitors with a rich sense of Spanish culture. For those who want to really see Spain, the city's fantastic heritage, vibrant artistic scene, and welcoming spirit make it unforgettable. Whether your interests are in supporting your preferred football club, seeing its well-known historical landmarks, or savoring its cuisine, Madrid offers something for everyone. Every traveler should give this city some thought.

CHAPTER 5:

BARCELONA:
Beaches, Gothic Adventures, and Vibrant Nights

Barcelona is among the most fascinating cities in Spain where modern life coexists peacefully with history, culture, and past. Barcelona sits near the Mediterranean Sea on the northeastern coast of Spain. It offers visitors a blend of a vibrant nightlife, winding Gothic streets, and sunny beaches. The vibrant city draws guests from all across the world, offering something for everyone—including art aficionados, architecture connoisseurs, beach enthusiasts, and party attendees. Barcelona is among the most fascinating and diverse destinations in Europe because of its rich history, outstanding landmarks, and energetic current culture. This section will look at Barcelona's finest, including its lovely beaches, the quaint sites in the Gothic district, and the energetic nightlife.

Beaches: Traveling to the Coast

Barcelona's lovely beach is among its strongest suits. The beaches of the city provide a peaceful haven where one may unwind and enjoy the ocean away from the hectic daily schedule. Barcelona's beaches are easily accessible, many just a short stroll from the city core. This makes it convenient for residents as well as visitors to savor the beautiful beaches and glistening clean waters connected with the Mediterranean.

Found in the bustling Barceloneta district, Barceloneta Beach is the most often used beach in Barcelona. Both residents and visitors like this beach, which has a vibrant scene with street vendors, fun bars, and palm palms. Perfect for sunbathing, swimming in the sea, or trying exciting water sports such jet skiing, paddleboarding, and windsurfing is Barceloneta. The beach is well known for its vibrant nightlife; numerous clubs and nightclubs along the beach front remain open late. The beach comes alive when the sun sets so that people may unwind and enjoy themselves in company.

Apart from Barceloneta, many other beaches around the coast provide various ambiance and experiences. Travelers seeking a quiet and leisureful experience might visit OCATA Beach in the neighboring town of EL MASNOU or Mar Bella and BOGATELL beaches, which provide tranquil waves and well-liked beach clubs. Anyone looking for a more sedate day by the sea, away from the crowded tourist places, would find these beaches to be very suitable. Barcelona's beaches reflect the way of life of the city and unite people of all ages to savor the Mediterranean pleasures, not just sunny areas.

Barcelona is committed to maintaining the excellent condition of its coast, therefore guaranteeing the cleanliness of its beaches and the availability of first-rate facilities. The clean urban beaches of the city include decent amenities like showers, chairs, and beach bars with cool beverages and regional cuisine. Barcelona is a beach destination you may visit any time as the Mediterranean climate means that most of the year Barcelona enjoys ideal weather for beach activities; lovely summers and moderate winters define this beach location.

Gothic Travels: Uncovering the Old Quarter

Barcelona's contemporary architecture and beach scene are well-known, but its meandering Gothic Quarter has a lot of history and culture. Barcelona's oldest section is the Gothic Quarter, or BARRI GÒTIC. Its little, meandering alleyways, historic houses, and secluded parks help visitors to feel as if they are in another era. Anyone visiting Barcelona has to see this lovely neighborhood. It allows you to investigate the rich cultural heritage of the city.

The magnificent Gothic architecture that stands out in the skyline of the old town is Barcelona Cathedral, which draws most attention from the Gothic Quarter. Among the outstanding specimens of Gothic architecture in Spain, the cathedral honors Santa Eulàlia, the patron saint of the city. The church's gorgeous interior, with soaring towers, intricate stained-glass windows, and magnificent shrines, is viewable to visitors. Another outstanding location is the courtyard of the church, home to several geese. It offers a peaceful respite from the congested outer streets. History and culture vultures may learn about the past of the city right in the chapel. Built beginning in the 13th century, it took many centuries to finish.

PLAÇA DEL REI, an antique plaza with old residences formerly occupied by the Catalan rulers, is part of the Gothic Quarter. The M USEU D'HISTORIA DE BARCELONA (Museum of the History of Barcelona) currently graces the square. Here visitors may learn about the Roman origins of the city and its historical developments. With its historic streets lined with charming cafés, little stores, and neighborhood pubs, walking through the Gothic Quarter seems like time travel. The area offers an interesting exploration of its meandering lanes. There are secret paths and hidden gardens that lead to unexpectedly valuable sites.

The Gothic Quarter's sense of surprise and curiosity is among its most endearing aspects. Its lanes will lead you to calm gardens, centuries-old buildings, and little street areas where time seems to stop. The Jewish community in ancient Barcelona concentrated in the region, known as El Call, the Jewish Quarter. Walking in this old neighborhood allows you to learn about the Jewish past of Barcelona and how it has shaped its varied culture.

A further significant location in the Gothic Quarter is PLAÇA SANT JAUME, a sizable plaza serving as the hub for municipal governance. Its two significant structures are the municipal hall, the AJUNTAMENT DE BARCELONA, and the PALAU DE LA GENERALITAT, home of the regional administration for Catalonia. The square is a crowded and significant area in the city as it holds many public events and gatherings.

Thrilling evenings: Barcelona's Enchantment at Night

Barcelona never sleeps; hence its nightlife is as diverse and fascinating as the city itself. With tapas restaurants, laid-back cafés, elegant nightclubs and rooftop pubs with breathtaking views, Barcelona has a vibrant nightlife. Both residents and visitors love this vivid scenario. At night, the city is alive and has plenty of entertainment choices. You could decide on a laid-back evening with beverages or a vibrant dance party running till early.

Barcelona's night scene is well-known for beginning late; most pubs and clubs are active until after midnight. The evening of the city is dispersed among many neighborhoods with unique ambiance. The creative aura of the El Born district is well known; trendy pubs and laid-back clubs selling beverages and highlighting live music. See Passeig de Gràcia if you want a more elegant encounter. There are some of the chicest rooftop bars in the city where you may sip beverages and savor breathtaking views of the cityscape and landmarks.

Particularly in the Barceloneta and PORT OLÍMPIC areas of Barcelona, a common party venue is close to the beach. For those wishing to dance to the newest sounds or relax by the sea with a drink in hand, visitors will find several beach clubs and pubs operating here until the early hours of the morning providing a vibrant environment. Popular for partygoers, the Opium Club close to PORT OLÍMPIC has worldwide DJs playing music till dawn.

Barcelona has a vibrant live music scene including many venues for both native and international events. Renowned throughout the city with live music events and DJ performances is the Razzmatazz club. Visitors looking for a closer experience should check the little pubs and clubs in El Raval and El POBLE-SEC, where local artists often perform indie rock, jazz, or traditional Catalan music.

Barcelona's nightlife is about spending time with people as much as about pubs and clubs. Perfect for hanging out with friends or meeting new people are the vibrant patios and outdoor spaces of the city. Young people also appreciate the Spanish custom of "BOTELLÓN," or public drinking, which lets them meet together and sip anything. Barcelona's nightlife offers incredible options for everyone's taste wherever you are in the city.

Barcelona combines the finest of many worlds: stunning beaches, century-old legacy, and a vibrant, always changing culture. Barcelona has something for everyone, from beach tanning to exploring the Gothic Quarter to the vibrant nightlife of the city. One of the most fascinating locations in Europe, its unique atmosphere will undoubtedly draw everyone who visits. Its blend of old-world elegance and contemporary life makes it Barcelona highlights the beauty and diversity of Spain by providing great beaches, interesting Gothic experiences, and vibrant nightlife.

CHAPTER 6:

THE ANDALUSIAN DREAM:
Seville, Córdoba, and Granada

Deep history, vibrant culture, and breathtaking landscape define Andalusia, in southern Spain. Three of Spain's well-known cities—Seville, Córdoba, and Granada—are found there. Every city presents one facet of the rich history and culture of the region. Uniquely formed by the Moors, Christian influences, and a blend of European and North African traditions, Andalusia is This mix produces a fascinating mix of contrasts wherein contemporary life coexists happily with history. Emphasizing its most well-known cities— Seville, Córdoba, and Granada—this chapter will examine the core of Andalusia. Every city shape Spain's history and culture significantly.

Seville: An Andalusian Heart

The energetic capital of Andalusia, Seville is One of the most appealing locations in Spain is this one with its rich history, elegant architecture, and vibrant environment. The city's palaces, castles, and streets—each displaying a tale of triumph, strength, and love—highlight the combination of Moorish, Gothic, and Renaissance designs. Flamenco evolved in Seville. Representing Andalusian culture, this vibrant and emotive dance is Everywhere in the city, the vibrant spirit of this art form is evident; music and dance abound on the streets and give the air life.

Seville's well-known church, the largest Gothic construction in the world, draws most visitors. Located where an ancient mosque had stood, this remarkable structure exhibits outstanding architectural design. Visitors may explore the many chambers adorned with holy art, stroll about the church's large interior with lofty columns, and appreciate its thorough outside. Once the pinnacle of a mosque, visiting the Giralda offers breathtaking views of the city. The Giralda stands for the significant Moorish legacy of Seville and its conversion into a Christian metropolis.

You absolutely should see the ALCÁZAR of Seville nearby. Built around the tenth century by the Moors, this exquisite mansion combines Islamic, Gothic, Renaissance, and Baroque elements. The serene environment created by the exquisite tilework, verdant gardens, and quiet paths helps visitors to feel as if they are returning into the period of Andalusian monarchy. Still a reminder of Seville's relevance today, the ALCÁZAR displays the creative and architectural excellence of its past.

Popular events among Seville, some of which are among the most well-known in Spain, reflect the vibrant culture of this city. Events like the Holy Week (Semana Santa) and the Seville Fair (Feria de Abril) evidence the strong traditions of the city. Parades and holy spirit abound throughout Holy Week as families and communities come together to honor their convictions. Featured flamenco dance, bullfighting, and brilliant parades adding thrills to the streets, the Feria de Abril is a joyful celebration of Andalusian culture. Seville's excitement, delight, and pride on these occasions help visitors to experience the vibrant nature of the city.

Seville's cuisine is quite crucial in portraying Andalusia's essence. The city is well-known for its tapas, little meals allowing visitors to savor the native cuisine. Among the mouthwatering cuisine Seville offers are fried fish, Iberian ham, SALMOREJO, cold tomato soup, and churros. These are several of the delicious Andalusian cuisine. Wonderful places to savor these classic dishes and soak in the energetic street scene are the many tapas bars in the city.

Córdoba: A City of Many Cultures and Variances

Once the seat of the Islamic Caliphate, Córdoba is a city that captures the unique mix of civilizations that throughout time have shaped Andalusia. Its history demonstrates how Muslims, Jews, and Christians have coexisted, mixing their traditions to produce a city that is both significant and beautiful. Rich in history, Córdoba has structures that tell tales of the strong forces and civilizations that formerly called there.

The Mezquita—that is, the Great Mosque of Córdoba—is the most well-known site in Córdoba. This remarkable structure reflects the Islamic past of the city and the great skill of the builders and artists who created it. The mosque has a large prayer hall with multiple horseshoe domes, each ornamented with soft red-and- white stripes. Its calm environment transports visitors to the time when Córdoba was a major Islamic cultural and learning hub. Combining two distinct architectural techniques, the Christian rulers erected a church within the mosque after they seized Córdoba. Strong emblem of the rich history of the city and how different civilizations have shaped their character, the Mezquita

A further significant location in Córdoba is the 14th-century fortress and palace known as ALCÁZAR DE LOS Reyes Cristianos, constructed by Christian rulers. Surrounded by lovely gardens and providing excellent views of the city, this famous structure was formerly the residence of Catholic royalty Ferdinand and Isabella. Calm gardens, Roman tiles, and ponds allowing visitors to witness how the city's lords lived help the ALCÁZAR to provide a peaceful haven from the crowded streets.

A significant historical site is Córdoba's JUDERÍA, Jewish Quarter. Here, the Jewish population of the city used to thrive. Visitors may walk the little lanes with white homes with typical courtyards nowadays. Showing the Jewish legacy of the city, the Synagogue of Córdoba is one of the few surviving ancient synagogues in Spain. The modest yet elegant architecture of the little temple reflects the dignity and elegance of the Jewish population in the city.

Beautiful public patios exposed to the annual Patio Festival (FIESTA DE LOS PATIOS) are another feature of Córdoba. People in the city outfit their backyards with flowers, plants, and ponds during this festival to create vibrant and cheerful scene. The patios depict the Andalusian way of life, in which daily life revolves much on family and society.

One knows Córdoba for its excellent cuisine. Popular meals that highlight the local tastes include SAL MORE JO, a thick tomato soup; FLAMENQUÍN, a fried pig meal; and RABO DE TORO, oxtail stew. Eating in Córdoba is unique. Along the city's gorgeous streets, visitors may savor traditional Andalusian cuisine in charming taverns and restaurants.

Granada: a city of palaces with Moorish past

At the foot of the Sierra Nevada mountains is the lovely and ancient city of Granada. The Alhambra, a magnificent palace and fortress, is Granada most renowned for. The city has rich cultural legacy and significant Moorish influence. Renowned throughout Spain, the Alhambra is considered as one of the finest specimens of Islamic architecture. Featuring elaborate arches, exquisite plaster work, and calm grounds with ponds and gardens, the palace is a lovely combination of Islamic art and architecture. Only its historical significance matches the splendor of the Alhambra as it was the final haven for the Moors in Spain before to their extinction in the fifteenth century.

Apart from the Alhambra, Granada has other significant sites including the Granada Cathedral and the Royal Chapel. Nestled close to the cathedral, the Royal Chapel marks the last resting place of Catholic monarch Ferdinand and Isabella. A significant historical and religious monument is the chapel's striking architecture and the graves of Spain's well-known royal couple. Highlighting the religious and cultural riches of the city, the Granada Cathedral has a magnificent Renaissance front and a spacious interior.

Renowned for its little lanes and white homes, Granada's ALVAICÍN neighborhood is a UNESCO World Heritage site highlighting the Moorish past of the city. Cobbled lanes in the area lead visitors through beautiful gardens and secret locations where jasmine smells abound. Particularly from the Mirador de San Nicolás, where one can see the palace with the Sierra Nevada mountains behind it, the ALVAICÍN boasts fantastic views of the Alhambra.

Food from Granada reflects her vibrant culture. Many foodies visit the city because of its well-known complimentary tapas with drink offer. Local cuisine is excellent and includes JAMÓN SERRANO (cured ham) and PIONONOS, a sweet treat. The crowded markets and city's classic pubs let you savor true Andalusian tastes.

Combining its history, culture, and beauty from the past and the present, the Andalusian dream is a journey into the core of Spain. Each of Seville, Córdoba, Granada has a unique tale. Granada is renowned for its breathtaking history; Seville is vibrant and full of energy; Córdoba is a blending of many civilizations. These towns, which concentrate Andalusia, provide visitors with the chance to visit a location where history is always evident. Every flamenco dance, mosque, and lunch you can sense the soul of the place. Traveling to Andalusia brings you to one of Spain's most breathtaking regions where you may savor the mild sunlight and create priceless memories.

CHAPTER 7:

SELF-GUIDED WALKING TOURS:
Explore Spain Like a Local

Walking is the ideal way to see Spain as it boasts a rich history, culture, and breathtaking surroundings. While self-directed walking tours provide a more intimate and free experience, guided outings are popular with visitors. These trips let visitors to appreciate the sense of Spain's cities, towns, and countryside free from tour group participation while exploring its attractions at their own pace. With enough preparation, you may locate unusual locations, enjoy everyday life, and create unforgettable moments in Spain like a native.

Why should one choose a self-guided walking tour?

Walking walks under self-guided direction provide a special sense of freedom and independence. You may proceed at your own pace, trust your emotions, and decide how long to remain at each location whether you are walking along the seaside in Barcelona or investigating the historic lanes of Madrid. This allows you to investigate Spain's culture more thoroughly free from the customary rush associated with group travel.

Self-guided walks also have the advantage of letting you personalize experience. Unlike planned group outings with a predetermined timetable, self-guided walking tours are adaptable to your own interests. Your path will be unique depending on your passion—art, architecture, history, cuisine, or environment. Given Spain's tiny size, one may quickly see several locations on one trip. Many cities include lovely parks, quaint neighborhoods, and historic historical sites.

Seeing the subtleties of daily life is a genuine and interesting opportunity available for you while strolling throughout Spain. You may unwind at a café for coffee, strike up friendly conversations with residents, or spend quiet time in a garden. Walking slowly allows you to discover beautiful streets, energetic marketplaces, and crowded squares hidden from view in automobiles or buses, therefore deepening your exploration of Spain.

How Should One Plan Their Own Walking Tour?

Here are some crucial things to consider for an enjoyable and effective self-guided walking tour in Spain. Selecting the places or regions of Spain you choose to visit marks the first stage in trip preparation. From the hectic capitals of Madrid and Barcelona to the ancient villages in Andalusia and the stunning Pyrenees, Spain has a varied range of locations. Every locality sees Spanish culture differently; hence it is crucial to choose locations that fit your preferences.

Start browsing for the finest walking trails after you have decided on your destinations. Clear walking paths and plans are available on various products including websites, apps, and guidebooks. Usually pointing out well-known sights like museums and historical monuments, these publications also include details on hidden treasures that residents find excellent value.

Consider combining well-known tourist destinations with less-known locations to provide a balanced trip emphasizing both well-known and hidden local attractions.

Planning also relies on timing. By geography, Spain's climate varies, scorching summers in the south and colder temperatures in the north. Particularly in southern cities like Seville or Granada, take your strolling walks early morning or late afternoon to be cool and avoid the heat. Plan your calendar carefully if you are heading in the summer as some stores and businesses might shut for a few hours in the afternoon for a break.

One should consider how one may go around the towns and cities of Spain. Public transit is decent in cities like Madrid and Barcelona, but walking is frequently the simplest and most enjoyable means of traveling around. Some locations, like finding out how to utilize the rail or bus systems, could need some additional preparation. Although moving around is often simpler in small towns and rural regions, it is still wise to pack a map or smartphone app to guide you.

- Choose your path depending on your preferred taste. Select locations that fit your interests, including local markets, art museums, historical landmarks, or lovely neighborhoods. Madrid, Barcelona, Seville, and Granada are among wonderful places for walking trips.

- Consult significant sites. Describe the key attractions of every city. Among them are the Alhambra in Granada, the Sagrada Família in Barcelona, and the Royal Palace in Madrid.

- Plan Walking Distances: Though the towns of Spain are simple to stroll in, consider the distances separating one location from another. Select walking routes that fit your speed considering factors such the temperature, break spots, and comfort level.

- Create a flexible travel plan; although the timetable is fantastic, it also includes time for unplanned leisure. Discover hidden gems, stroll through beautiful neighborhoods, and stop at little stores or cafés as you go.

- Wear comfortable Shoes: The various surfaces and gravel streets of Spain call for you to choose supportive and comfortable shoes. Select shoes suitable for many kinds of terrain and extended walks.

- Take pauses and eat lengthy dinners are typical in Spain Rest as you stroll at local cafés for coffee, nibbles, or a cold drink.

- Take stops for pictures; Spain has attractive squares, architectural wonders, and energetic streets. Go slowly; pause and appreciate the beauty of the locations you visit.

- Visit Local Markets and Shops: Perfect for experiencing local culture in Spain are La BOQUERIA in Barcelona and Mercado de San Miguel in Madrid. See these locations for unique cuisine, mementos, and cultural encounters.

- Consider the time of the day. Early in the morning will help you to avoid the heat and the crowds, particularly in summer. Early morning silence in many locations is ideal for photo and exploration purposes.

- To assist you move between venues and avoid being lost, use a map or GPS app. Should you lose mobile service, you may download maps for use offline.

- Honor local norms and etiquette. Respect regional traditions, particularly at sites of religion or culture. Dress correctly and abide by guidelines for photographing or acting at certain locations.

- Add Scenic Routes: Charming streets and breathtaking scenery abound in Spain. In cities like Barcelona, choose routes along the coastline or through parks (like Park GÜELL).

- Remember to have lunch and pauses for relaxation. Lunch in Spain often falls between two and four PM, which is a wonderful time to unwind and embrace the habit of nap-taking. Spend a break at a neighboring restaurant savoring regional cuisine such paella, gazpacho, or tapas.

- Drink plenty of water; Spain, particularly in the summer, can become really hot. Remember to drink water; bring a water bottle particularly if you are traveling a great distance or if the sun is really strong.

- Use Walking Tour Apps: A few cities have self-guided walking tours available via apps. These applications enhance your trip by providing you with audio information on historical sites and cultural venues.

- Look at accessibility: If you have mobility problems, choose simple routes and places before you go. While certain older districts might be challenging to traverse, many Spanish municipalities are striving to simplify travel for everybody.

- Consider going on guided walking excursions to deepen your knowledge. If you like professional insights, consider combining your own finds with a well-planned walking tour. About architecture, history, and culture, guides may provide you with insightful material.

- Bring only what you need, drink, sunscreen, and a light jacket—not overkills. Pack sparingly; too much will slow you down. Instead choose a little, cozy bag.

- Travel long distances on public transport. While touring is best done on foot, Spain's public transportation is very trustworthy. Long distance travel between locations may be done on the trams, buses, or metro.

- Many Spanish cities are vibrant at evening with distinctive atmosphere and strong lighting. It is much different to walk in the evenings beside the river or across plazas.

- Go at the local tempo: Spain leads a relaxed lifestyle. Do not rush on your stroll. Rather, slow down to absorb the surroundings, watch people, and appreciate Spain's leisurely pace of life.

Finding Madrid: A Self-Guided Trek throughout the Capital

Madrid, Spain's energetic capital, is a fantastic city for solo, foot-based exploration. Madrid is well-known for its vivid atmosphere, exquisite architecture, and rich past. There are many of walking routes there, allowing you to discover hidden gems as well as well as well-known attractions.

Start your walking trip at the well-known Puerta del Sol area in Madrid's middle. From here, you may explore the adjacent Plaza Mayor, a large area bursting with elegant architecture and bustling cafés. See the Royal Palace, home of the Spanish royal family, as you tour Madrid's historic core. The enormous gardens and fade of the palace are remarkable; the surrounding Almudena Cathedral accentuates the beauty of the location.

Fans of art should not miss the "Golden Triangle of Art." Spanish and international art is quite abundant in these three museums: The Prado Museum, the Reina Sofía Museum, and the Thyssen-Bornemisza Museum. Although these are well-known landmarks, you might also visit Retiro Park nearby. Locals visit this peaceful, grassy area to unwind and savor the outdoors.

After a day of sight-seeing, go to the La Latina area—known for its vibrant evenings and tapas bars. This area is perfect for a leisurely stroll down little streets lined with historic buildings where one may have a snack and a glass of wine. See the Mercado de San Miguel, a hive of food markets offering fresh seafood, salted meats, cheeses, and desserts.

Discovering Barcelona: A Stroll Through Mediterranean Beauty and Modernist Wonders

Barcelona is a fantastic city for a self-guided walking trip; it is well known for its Mediterranean flair and contemporary architecture. Beginning your trip in the Gothic Quarter, little, winding lanes lead to secluded parks and historic structures. See the lovely Gothic Barcelona Cathedral and savor the atmosphere of this ancient region.

From the Gothic Quarter, go toward La Rambla, the bustling strolling avenue right in Barcelona's center. You will find little stores, street performers, and bustling marketplaces. Wander to the most well-known market in Spain, the MERCAT de Sant Josep de la BOQUERIA, on a side excursion. Here you could sample traditional Catalan cuisine, salty meats, and fresh fruits.

Barcelona is mostly known for the creations of builder Antoni Gaudí, whose distinct style permeates the whole city. Start with the well-known Sagrada Família, incomplete creation of art by Gaudí drawing visitors from all across the world. Then stop at PARK GÜELL, a public park bursting with Gaudí's imaginative creations and breathtaking city vistas.

Do not miss the Eixample neighborhood, which is noted for its contemporary architecture, when strolling around Barcelona. Two of Gaudí's most well-known creations exhibiting his inventive ideas are Casa BATLLÓ and Casa MILÀ, often known as La Pedrera. The Eixample's wide streets are ideal for a leisurely stroll so you can take in the lovely architecture and energetic atmosphere of the neighborhood.

See the Barceloneta neighborhood to really appreciate Barcelona's Mediterranean splendor. One of the many beach bars will let you relax; you may stroll along the shore, have fresh seafood at a restaurant by the water. This neighborhood is among the favorites of the city because of the lovely beaches, mild Mediterranean breezes, and energetic streets.

Investigating Andalusia: Granada, Seville, Córdoba

A historic region, Andalusia's cities—Seville, Córdoba, and Granada—offer some of Spain's most exquisite and culturally fascinating strolling experiences. Starting your adventure in Seville, a city known for flamenco dance and exquisite architecture, your journey begins in the gorgeous ALCÁZAR of Seville, a castle with exquisitely landscaped gardens and adorned halls. Proceed next to Seville church, the largest Gothic church in the world. For excellent city views, climb the Giralda Tower.

Wander leisurely around the historic Jewish Quarter of Córdoba, which has white homes, little streets, and lovely gardens. See the spectacular mosque turned church known as Mezquita, a UNESCO World Heritage site. Beautiful views of the Guadalquivir River abound from the Roman Bridge of the city; the ALCÁZAR de Los Reyes Cristianos exhibits a slice of Córdoba's past.

Granada is the perfect spot for your individual exploration with its Moorish background and breathtaking vistas of the Sierra Nevada mountains. Though you should most certainly see the Alhambra, make sure you also explore the ALVAICÍN. Little streets, white homes, and breathtaking vistas of the Alhambra define this medieval Moorish region. One famous site to see the Alhambra with mountains in the backdrop is the Mirador de San Nicolás.

Self-guided walking tours enable you explore Spain at your own pace, thus savoring the natural beauty, history, and culture of this wonderful nation. For those who visit Spain's vibrant capitals, Madrid and Barcelona as well as its ancient monuments in Andalusia, it has numerous advantages. This nation offers chances for roaming, learning, and experiencing the native way of life. Whether your trip to Spain is first-time or seasoned, strolling around the nation allows you to really appreciate it in a manner that bus tours or automobile excursions cannot equal. Put on your walking shoes, make a schedule, and be ready to see Spain like a native.

CHAPTER 8:

EATING YOUR WAY THROUGH SPAIN:
From Tapas to Paella

Spain is wonderful to eat as well as to look at. The nation has a rich gastronomic legacy shaped by its many regions, climate, and cultures; each adds distinct flavor and cooking techniques to the national cuisine. From little nibbles in little bars to lavish feasts from local chefs, Spanish cuisine is a major component of the culture and experience of the nation. Whether you are savoring a large dinner or a little dish of olives, dining in Spain offers a great approach to learn about its traditions, history, and cuisine.

The universe of tapas: little dishes with great tastes

One of the most well-known dishes in Spain, tapas are impossible to miss while visiting the country. These tiny meals are unbelievably delicious. Originally little appetizers presented with beverages to cover a glass of wine or sherry and prevent flies, tapas originated in Andalusia. Over time, the tapas habit has evolved and grown to be significant for Spanish cuisine. Today's tapas range from simple appetizers like olives and cheese to more sophisticated cuisine including fish, meats, and vegetables.

The fact that tapas are supposed to be shared makes them among the greatest as it lets you savor several flavors in one dinner. Usually with a drink of local wine, beer, or sherry, residents of Spain enjoy tapas in a laid-back and convivial environment at pubs and restaurants. Depending on the locale, these little dinners might vary significantly and promote local cuisine and goods and cooking techniques.

In Andalusia, you might sample grilled prawns (gambas a la plancha), cured ham from Spain, or SALMOREJO, a cold tomato soup. Pintxos are beloved little sliced treats found in the Basque Country. Popular kinds of tapas usually consist of fish, meat, or unusual combinations of regional cuisine. Popular appetizers at Madrid traditional taverns include CALLOS A LA MADRILEÑA (a thick tripe stew) and tortilla ESPAÑOLA (a Spanish egg with potatoes and onions).

Apart from their flavor, tapas are fun as they unite people. To have a delightful adventure known as a tapas crawl—where they visit many places and sample a new dish at each— Spaniards commonly congregate with friends or relatives. It is a laid-back and leisureful approach to sample several cuisines while soaking in the energetic vibe of Spain's districts.

Paella: The Old Spanish Dish

Without discussing paella, no element of Spanish cuisine would be complete. From Valencia, this well-known meal captures Spain's culinary customs. Usually cooked in a broad, shallow pan over an open flame, paella is a rice-based meal. With various variations dependent on the locale and available ingredients, the meal is well-known for its vivid colors, good flavors, and adaptability.

Considered the "original" Valencian paella, it consists of chicken, rabbit, and sometimes fish along with vegetables and saffron, which lends a golden hue. Usually prepared in a delicious sauce, the rice takes up the taste of the veggies and spices.

Although Valencian paella is a staple meal in Spanish cuisine, there are other variations all throughout the nation that highlight the range of Spanish cookery. Fresh fish, prawns, mussels, and clams make up seafood paella, which is extremely popular in coastal cities like Barcelona. Seafood paella from southern Spain could have langoustines, squid, and crab. Paella de VERDURÁS (vegetable paella), which adds fresh, seasonal vegetables such artichokes, peas, and bell peppers, may be preferred in the landlocked parts of Spain.

Usually, paella is served with friends and family seated around a large, hot pan. Whether in a tiny town at a fair or at a seaside restaurant, this meal unifies people and is a symbol of celebration. Cooking paella lets the rice acquire taste and shape by means of time and attention. This reveals Spain's approach of savoring food: spending time to appreciate the flavor and cooking technique every mouthful presents.

JAMÓN IBÉRICO: Spanish Ham's Craft

Without sampling the well-known smoked ham, a staple of Spanish cuisine, no gastronomy trip of Spain is complete. Among the greatest hams in the world is JAMÓN IBÉRICO. It originates from black Iberian pigs housed in the DEHESA, a region of Spain including extensive oak forests. The pigs consume nuts, which give the ham a distinctive appearance with fat marbling and taste great.

JAMÓN IBÉRICO exists in many grades. JAMÓN IBÉrico de bellota is the greatest quality name. Pigs that can roam freely and eat only acorns in the autumn make this. Depending on the kind of ham, the curing process takes a lengthy period—usually two to four years. The outcome is a smooth and delicious meal with a good combination of spicy and salty tastes.

Usually presented in thin slices in Spain, JAMÓN IBÉRICO emphasizes its great flavor. Usually eaten with a glass of Spanish red wine or sherry, it is also a snack by itself. JAMÓN is also often accompanied with various Spanish cheeses, olives, and toasted bread. Local ham stores known as JAMONERÍAS abound around Spain, where you may sample many types of ham and see expertly sliced pieces of meat.

The daily schedule of eating. Spanish cuisine culture revolves mostly around JAMÓN. In certain spots, you might see full JAMÓN legs hanging in tapas restaurant windows, just waiting to be cut, and presented to eager customers. Consider visiting a nearby JAMÓN facility or planning a structured trip if you want a true experience. This allows you to discover the background of this well-known Spanish cuisine as well as its preparation techniques.

Chocolate-Based Churros: Sweet Spanish Custom

Many visitors believe that experiencing the iconic Spanish breakfast or dessert, churros con chocolate, completes a journey to Spain. Inside these fried dough snacks are soft; outside they are crispy. Usually served with thick, creamy hot chocolate for dipping, they are Though the technique of fried dough has been around ancient times and has evolved over the years into the delicious delicacy we enjoy today, churros are usually connected to Spain.

Made with only flour, water, and salt, churros are straightforward. The dough is formed with a star-shaped tip and deep-fried until golden brown. Served with a little cup of sweeter, thicker than what you often get in other countries thick hot chocolate, they are topped with sugar and sometimes cinnamon. Particularly in the colder months when the warm chocolate tastes great, people in Spain sometimes have churros with chocolate for morning.

Though each region has its own special interpretation of this iconic dessert, churros are extremely popular all throughout Spain. Usually tall and straight, churros are found in Madrid PORRAS, or thicker and fluffier churros, abound throughout Andalusia. One of the greatest places to savor churros is at a CHURRERÍA, a dedicated store offering this beloved delicacy. Before beginning their day, locals often gather in the morning to enjoy churros with friends and catch-up over a hot cup of cocoa.

Wine and cider: Liquid jewels from Spain

Wine and cider are well-known from Spain. One cannot completely appreciate a national cuisine tour without sampling some of the finest beverages. There are many types of wine in the nation, and every region creates their own distinctive styles using native grapes and soil. Each of the well-known wine regions, La Rioja, Ribera del Duero, and Priorat—offers a unique experience for wine AFICIONERS.

Strong flavors, superb balance of acidity, and how well Spanish wines complement food are well-known features of their quality. Rioja red wines are well-known for their rich tastes; RÍAS BAIXAS white wines are valued for their fresh, unassuming taste. Though it is also well-known for cava, a sparkling wine from Catalonia, and sidra, a cider used in the Basque Country and Asturias, Spain is most recognized for wine. Usually poured from high up to mix in air, sidra enhances flavor by means of air. Many people like it with hearty soups or snacks.

Like many facets of Spanish cuisine, wine and cider are best savored when shared with others. These beverages fit the vibrant culinary scene of the nation whether you are savoring a crisp cider at a neighborhood cider business or a glass of wine at a beach restaurant.

Eating in Spain connects one with the traditions, history, and culture of the nation rather than just the cuisine. From little tapas to large bowls of paella and including well-known delicacies like JAMÓN IBÉRICO and mouthwatering churros with chocolate, Spanish cuisine has a fantastic blend of flavors and textures. These recipes highlight the many parts of the nation and diverse culinary customs. Spain's cuisine will surely influence you regardless of your level of familiarity with food or simply a visitor eager to sample fresh tastes. Bring your tummy and be ready to savor your path of Spanish cuisine!

CHAPTER 9:

SPAIN'S DRINKING CULTURE:
Sangria, Wine, and Local Cocktails

In Spain, drinking is quite significant in daily life. It captures local conventions, history, and the present of the nation. Drinking in Spain goes beyond just savoring a bottle of wine on a sunny day or commemorating local events. A significant element of the dining experience is a social activity and a meaningful custom. Like its landscape, Spain's drinking scene is energetic and diverse. It features well-known Rioja wines as well as cool summertime delicious sangrias. This chapter will look at Spain's traditional drinking culture, stressing sangria, wine, and well-known local beverages that are vital to social and gastronomic events there.

Sangria: Spain's Notable Celebration Beverage

When people think of Spain, most commonly they see sangria as the first beverage. Popular during summer afternoons in Spain and during happy get-togethers, this fruity drink is not entirely understood by many people about its history and significance in Spanish society. Made with red wine, diced fruit, sugar, and sometimes extra additives like brandy or soda water, sangria is Usually presented in large pitchers or bowls to share, this drink is perfect for social events and should be enjoyed with others.

Sangria started in Spain, where many regions created their unique varieties of this beverage depending on their history of winemaking. Though this notion has been around for years, mixing wine with fruits and spices is mostly recognized in Spanish cuisine. Including the Romans, many civilizations have created their own variants. In Spain, Sangria evolved into the drink of choice we know today. Beginning to be produced in larger quantities for events and gatherings, modern sangria gained popularity in the 18th and 19th centuries.

Red wine combined with fruits like oranges, lemons, apples, and berries forms Sangria mostly. Certain recipes could call for added ingredients like whiskey, rum, or fizzy water for some bubbles in certain regions. Usually chilled, the drink is an excellent choice for sizzling summer days in Spain—especially in Andalusia, where it can become really scorching.

Though it is becoming increasingly common in pubs and restaurants all around, Sangria still has great connections to Spanish culture and custom. Usually at home, individuals in Spain share it with family and friends, particularly at family get-togethers, celebrations, and fairs. This is a symbol of camaraderie and happiness; this drink breaks the ice and pulls people together. Though you may drink several variations of Sangria all year, it is usually associated with summer. One can match the seasons with fruits, wine, and spices.

Spanish Wine: A Terroir Celebration

Spain is among the first and most revered nations for producing wine; drinking customs there revolve on this beverage. The nation has more than seventy wine regions, each with unique qualities and flavors. The many grape varieties, terrain, and weather patterns scattered around the Iberian Peninsula define this variety. From well-known locations like Rioja and the sunny hills of Andalusia, Spain has several distinct wines. These wines highlight how closely Spain's terrain and long tradition of wine production define her.

Particularly Tempranillo grape red wines are the most often consumed in Spain. Particularly from the Rioja region, Tempranillo grape wines offer great, deep tastes with traces of dark fruits, tobacco, and spices. Usually housed in oak barrels, these wines provide greater taste and richness to the beverage. Rioja is a well-known wine region in Spain distinguished for its mouthwatering wines with a harmonic combination of refinement and strength. People all over appreciate these wines. Along with many other wine-producing regions in Spain, like Ribera del Duero, Priorat, and the PENEDÉS region, each with its own distinct style, are

Especially the ALBARIÑO grape from the RÍAS BAIXAS region in Galicia, one of the most well-known white wine varieties in Spain, Spanish white wines are worth tasting. Taste of lemon, green apple, and flowers; ALBARIÑO wines are light, fresh, aromatic. Common cuisine in coastal parts of Spain, seafood is often accompanied with this wine. Another excellent white wine from Rueda is the Verdejo. Perfect for sizzling summer days, its flavor is fresh and crisp.

Legal control over the unique age grading system used in Spanish wines controls their Among the categories this approach offers are Crianza, RESERVA, and Gran RESERVA. These labels indicate the length of oak barrel and bottle aging for wine. Whereas RESERVA wines must mature for at least three years, including one year in oak barrels—Crianza wines must age for at least two years. Gran RESERVA wines spend two years in wood barrels in addition to a minimum of five years of aging. Aging wine brings more complex and deeper tastes. Selecting a Crianza, RESERVA, or Gran RESERVA depends on personal preferences and the context.

In Spain, wine is not merely a drink; it is also a major component of social life and often drank with meals. Family meals, get-togethers with friends, and even big events like fairs and weddings all have wine as a staple. Special wine rituals like wine tastings and farm visits abound in certain parts of Spain. These events enable visitors to experience some of the greatest wines in the nation and learn about wine making.

Local Drinks: From Horchata to Tinto de Verano

Apart from sangria and wine, Spain has other regional beverages highlighting its vibrant drinking scene. Easy to prepare and ideal for hot weather or any celebration, these beverages include

TINTO DE VERANO is a quite well-known beverage in Spain, particularly in summer. Red wine mixed with lemon soda or sparkling water produces this simple and reviving beverage. Perfect for warm days is this light and sparkling drink. T INTO DE VERANO is "summer red wine." Particularly in Madrid, where you can get it on patios and in bars, this drink is quite common in Spain.

Another beloved beverage is the REBUJITO, which is well-known in southern Spain particularly during the exciting Feria de Abril in Seville. Made with manzanilla, a kind of dry sherry from SANLÚCAR de Barrameda, combined with soda water, the REBUJITO is a beverage. It is served on ice along with some lemon. Perfect for hot, lively days in the Andalusian heat, this drink is pleasant and simple to consume. Usually consumed with tapas or fish, the REBUJITO has evolved as a symbol of Andalusian revelry.

Both residents and visitors of Spain enjoy certain distinctive non-alcoholic beverages. Horchata de chufa is a well-known drink. Made from Valencia's tiger nuts, which are sweet and creamy, this drink is Usually cold, horchata is served with a soft bread known as a FARTON, which is dipped into the beverage. Families particularly on sizzling summer days find great popularity for this cold drink.

Spanish Social Courtesy

Drinking is often a social activity in Spain, and the manner individuals drink reveals how much they value hanging out and having fun with others. Whether it is purchasing a round at a bar or savoring a bottle of wine with family at dinner, people really love sharing beverages in Spain. Friends or relatives may order several beverages or a bottle of wine so everyone may sample and appreciate the tastes together.

Usually laid back, Spanish bars let customers concentrate more on having fun with one other than on formality. Usually consumed with wine or cocktails, tapas are little nibbles. The concept of "IR DE TAPAS" is fundamental in many spheres of Spain and shapes social life. Having a drink and a little meal at every pub, people go from one to another.

Maintaining late hours is another essential component of Spanish drinking customs. Especially in large cities like Madrid and Barcelona, Spaniards often eat supper and drink late—usually beginning around 9 or 10 p.m. Many folks visit pubs or clubs for extra drinks after supper; sometimes they remain out until early morning.

Deeply ingrained customs and a rich and diverse drinking culture define Spain from the sweet taste of sangria to the premium wines of Rioja and the revitalizing native cocktails like TINTO DE VERANO and REBUJITO, Spain has a wide selection of beverages. The range of beverages is as varied as the stunning landscape of this nation. Spain's drinking scene celebrates togetherness, leisure, and enjoyment whether your drink is horchata on a sizzling summer day, a pitcher of sangria with friends, or wine at a neighborhood bar.

CHAPTER 10:

STAYING LIKE A LOCAL:
The Best Places to Sleep in Spain

Spain offers several lodging options fit for all types of visitors from its vibrant cities, rich history, and diversified landscapes. Beyond standard tourist hotels, one should search for more authentic and unusual locations to stay in order to fully experience Spanish culture and explore the nation like a native. Spain provides something for you regardless of your preferred scene—the peaceful countryside, the bustling metropolis, or the seaside. This chapter will explore some fantastic lodging options in Spain, ranging from hip hostels to small boutique hotels, rural escapes to seaside resorts.

Conventions Spanish Hotels: Combining Comfort and Charm

Spain has a lot of traditional eateries offering coziness, history, and a flavor of local culture. Generally speaking, these locations provide a more individualized and intimate experience than large multinational hotel chains. Many classic hotels are housed in historical castles, former temples, royal palaces, and other architectural relics. They enable visitors to enjoy contemporary conveniences while also experiencing history.

Many wonderful boutique hotels displaying the local architecture and culture abound in Madrid, Seville, and Barcelona. Typically featuring exquisite old-style elements such elegant tile patterns, oak beams, and classic Spanish gardens, these hotels Usually emphasizing presenting visitors with a home-away-from- home feel, the service is polite and welcoming. Remaining at one of these classic hotels allows you to enjoy excellent Spanish culture and experience local way of life.

Many of these venerable hotels are also in key locations, which makes walking around the city simple. For instance, staying in a modest hotel in the Santa Cruz district in Seville puts you at a short distance from the renowned ALCÁZAR Palace and Seville Cathedral. Staying in a Gothic Quarter hotel in Barcelona will allow you to explore little streets, discover hidden plazas, and see the city's blend of modern and historic architecture.

PARADORES: Visit Spain's Historic Monasteries and Castles

Consider vacationing in a parador to experience Spain really and uniquely. Fancy hotels called PARADORES are housed in old buildings like palaces, temples, castles, and convents. Starting the PARADORES de Turismo de España network in the 1920s, the Spanish government sought to promote travel to off-the-beaten-path locations and preserve Spain's architectural legacy.

Around the nation, there are more than ninety PARADORES that provide a special blend of contemporary comfort, history, and culture. Sleeping in a parador allows you to relax in renowned and lovely locations across Spain.

Usually situated in stunning locations like mountains, hills, or near the sea, these houses enable people to relate with the heritage of the region and provide wonderful vistas.

Located in the northern parts of Spain, some of the most well-known PARADORES are the Parador de Santiago de Compostela in Galicia, housed in a former royal hospital and just steps from the renowned Santiago de Compostela Cathedral, or the Parador de GIJÓN in Asturias, a 16th-century castle overlooking the Bay of Biscay. The Parador de Carmona in Andalusia is in an antique Moorish castle with excellent views of the landscape. Rising above the breathtaking El Tajo Gorge, the Parador de Ronda offers spectacular views of the surroundings.

Recognized for their great comfort and service, PARADORES also actively save Spain's architectural and cultural legacy. While enjoying the conveniences of a contemporary hotel, staying in a parador allows you to explore Spain's history.

Rural Retreats & Agrotourism: Discover Spain's countryside

Think about visiting rural regions and engaging in agrotourism if you want to escape the hectic city life and appreciate a calmer pace in Spain. This offers an excellent approach to enjoy local customs and the surroundings. Beautiful rural hotels, country homes, and agrotourism sites abound throughout Spain. Here visitors may unwind in a serene environment surrounded by contemporary conveniences.

Staying in a CORTijo, a classic Andalusian house, is a terrific approach to appreciate Spain's countryside. Many of these rural houses have become boutique hotels, offering visitors a peaceful and lovely place to stay. Living in a CORTijO allows you to savor simple rural life among olive orchards, farms, and hills in a stunning location.

Country hotels stress organic farming and sustainability abound in locations such Castilla-La Mancha, Extremadura, and the Balearic Islands. These hotels let visitors taste locally sourced cuisine and learn about nearby agricultural methods. To appreciate the stunning Spanish landscape, these locations often offer entertaining events such wine tasting, horseback riding, and walks.

Apart from CORTIJOS, Spain has several rural guesthouses and bed-and-breakfasts offering a closer view of country life. Many of these family-owned businesses provide visitors with handmade cuisine, a pleasant greeting, and chances to interact with the surrounding community. Staying in a rural hotel is a terrific opportunity to relax from the demands of contemporary life and allow you to enjoy actual Spanish town life.

Beachfront Resorts to Visit: Oceanic Sleeping

Beautiful coastlines abound in Spain, from Atlantic seas of Galicia to Mediterranean beaches of Costa Brava. Living in a hotel or rental close by the coast will help you to really appreciate Spain if you prefer the beach.

There are many of waterfront hotels, spas, and homes with magnificent views of the sea around the Costa Brava, Balearic Islands, and Canary Islands. Whether a visitor is seeking reasonably priced beach alternatives or luxury, these locations are fit for all kinds of guests. Remaining at a waterfront hotel allows you to enjoy the breathtaking views of the Atlantic or Mediterranean Ocean along with the calming sound of waves accompanying your trip.

Unlike the large international resorts, numerous little hotels and resorts offering a laid-back and intimate environment exist in areas such as Mallorca and Ibiza. Many of these locations are quiet, distant from crowded regions, so you may appreciate the sea's splendor without disturbance. Usually, it includes outdoor pools, beach bars and patios where one may relax and take in the surroundings.

For a more opulent experience, Spain has many chic resorts and private homes by the sea. Beautiful houses with secluded beach access, personal chefs, and expansive outdoor space abound in Marbella and Costa Brava. Anyone seeking a more intimate and pleasant encounter would find these chic locations perfect.

Hostels & Boutique Guesthouses: Chic Affordable Housing

Spain features various hostels and little guesthouses if your vacation budget is tight, or you seek a laid-back atmosphere. These locations provide an inexpensive and unique approach to take in the nation. The hostels in Spain have become really better recently. They are increasingly sought after by young visitors and hikers as they provide chic and cozy lodging with contemporary amenities.

Many cities like Barcelona, Madrid, and Granada offer hostels to fit varying tastes and budgets. With big public areas, private rooms, and varied social activities like group dinners and guided city visits, some hostels offer a contemporary, modern vibe. These hostels allow visitors to meet other travelers and exchange tales about their trip in Spain.

Private guesthouses are an excellent option if you want a more cozy and intimate stay. Usually featuring well designed rooms, friendly hosts, and a laid-back atmosphere, these small, independent establishments Sleeping at a modest hotel allows you to see the surroundings more like a local. Usually, the hosts like offering advice on the greatest views and activities around.

There are many fantastic sites in Spain that each visitor would find suited for their tastes and wishes for sleeping. Whether your preferred lodging is a contemporary hostel in the city, a tranquil area in the countryside, a luxury hotel housed in a historic structure, Spain has a range of options. There is something for everyone. Staying in areas displaying the local way of life can help you to have a more authentic and considerable experience in Spain. Spain is a fantastic spot to stay and make lifelong memories whether your trip is to the energetic cities of Madrid and Barcelona, savors the beaches of the Balearic Islands, or lounges in the peaceful Andalusia countryside.

CHAPTER 11:

The Essential Packing Guide
for Your Spain Adventure

Spain is a wonderful country to visit with its varied landscape, rich history, and energetic cities. Whether your vacation to Spain calls for seeing historical monuments in Seville, enjoy the sunny Costa Brava, or explore the crowded streets of Madrid, you should pack appropriately. It will be simpler and more pleasant for you to enjoy Spain's varied weather, culture, and everyday activities if you dress appropriately, use appropriate accessories, and pack necessary travel gear. This section provides a comprehensive packing guide to assist with your travel to Spain.

Acquiring Knowledge about Spain's Climate

Before you start packing for your vacation to Spain, be aware of the diverse weather patterns seen there. Though your location will affect the weather, Spain has a Mediterranean climate. Though the temperature varies between the coast, the middle, and the north, Spain typically boasts pleasant and dry weather with scorching summers and moderate winters.

While winters are moderate with usual temperatures around 10°C (50°F), summer temperatures in beach locations such Barcelona, Valencia, and Málaga may soar beyond thirty (86°F). Summers are hot in central locations like Madrid and winters are frigid. While winter temperatures might dip below freezing, summer temperatures could soar above 35°C (95°F. Particularly in the autumn and winter, the northern regions—including Bilbao and Galicia—get more rain and milder temperature. Although the Canary Islands and Balearic Islands enjoy pleasant year-round temperatures, summer may be hot.

Remember to pack with consideration for the local climate of the destination. If you are heading summer wise, dress in light clothing. Wear cozy jackets if you are on a winter trip. Whether you are traveling in the heat of the day or confronting chilly evenings, be sure to bring adaptable gear that lets you respond to changing weather conditions.

Clothes: Choosing Comfort and Fashion

Spain's fashionable population is well-known; hence appearance is quite important in their culture. While touring the nation, your comfort should come first as you will be walking a lot on scenic ocean walks or rocky paths. Choosing light and adaptable attire will enable you to suit the local fashion and satisfy your trip's pragmatic demands.

It is advisable to prepare outfits including items that may be mixed in many ways. Every wardrobe fits neutral hues like black, white, blue, and brown. With only a few pieces, women may choose to pack many dresses, skirts, and shirts that would readily convert from daily wear to evening wear. Spain is well-known for its fashionable street wear. Thus, try to seem nice and well put together even if you are clothing casually. For day-time touring, pack a pair of cozy shoes—such as chic sneakers or cozy boots. These will look good and keep you cozy on lengthy treks.

Spanish society promotes a finer fashion in the evenings. Women might select a fitting top or a lovely dress along with clean trousers. Men could dress in a polo or casual shirt with modern jeans or trousers. Summertime packing light and flexible textiles like cotton or linen makes sense. Coverage of your clothes is crucial in the colder months. Particularly in Madrid, where winter evenings may turn chilly, a decent jacket or coat is vital. Particularly in northern regions where it rains often, it is a clever idea to pack a lightweight rain jacket or waterproof coat as the weather changes fast.

Remember to bring your clothing if you want to visit Spanish beaches. Perfect for swimming or sunbathing, Spain has some of Europe's most stunning beaches. From the beach to a café or restaurant, a cover-up or sarong helps you get. If you are heading to a more elegant beach club, consider packing a nicer dress or lovely swimwear to complement the atmosphere there.

Shoes: Stylish and Comfortable Choices

When visiting Spain, one should choose comfortable shoes. You will spend a lot of time strolling through the beautiful streets of cities like Barcelona and Seville, walking on beaches, or seeing old sites. Plan your vacation and make sure you pack fashionable but comfortable shoes.

Wearing comfortable shoes is crucial if you want to explore and stroll leisurely on Cobblestone streets. Spanish cities often have steep streets and uneven walkways, hence choosing robust shoes with sufficient support can assist prevent blisters and maintain your comfort. Choose flexible shoes, such as chic sneakers, fit for nighttime trips and daily activities.

You may want climbing shoes if you want to explore natural reserves or rural regions. Mountains and national parks abound in Spain where one may enjoy outdoor pursuits like climbing and environmental exploration. For these treks, strong, waterproof climbing boots are a wise buy.

You want comfortable but fashionable shoes for evenings out or special occasions. Women may choose to pack a pair of elegant flats or shoes fit for both semi-formal and laid-back events. Men's choice of leather flats or casual dress shoes will depend on the kind of the venue or occasion they are attending.

Accessories: Fashionable and Practical Extraverts

Accessories enhance your wardrobe and are also crucial for your comfort and convenience while visiting Spain. Particularly if you are visiting outdoor locations, a decent pair of sunglasses help to shield your eyes from the strong Mediterranean sun. Get a decent set of sunglasses that suit many outfits and prevent UV light.

Particularly in the summer, a wide-brimming cap or hat will shield you from the sun. When you are outside, at the beach or on a rural hike, this is beneficial. Particularly in colder seasons or while visiting holy sites requiring modesty, a scarf or shawl is a valuable tool for both fashion and comfort.

One finds wonderful use from a shoulder bag or daypack. Choose a little, cozy bag to carry your phone, camera, sunscreen, water bottle and camera. Because it securely secures your items and frees your hands, a compact backpack or shoulder bag is ideal. Using a bag with anti-theft elements can help you to keep your stuff secure whether you are visiting significant sites like the Sagrada Familia in Barcelona or the Alhambra in Granada.

A travel wallet or money belt is a handy tool to pack for your trip in Spain. While you are visiting the nation, this may aid guarding your credit cards, passport, and other vital documents. To avoid loss, it is smart to have numerous secure places to store your pricey belongings, especially in crowded tourist destinations.

Personal Care and Toiletries

Do not overlook packing your personal care and amenities while preparing for your vacation to Spain. They will enable you to remain hygienic and fresh throughout your vacation. Although Spain has a lot of personal care products available in stores, it is wise to pack your own basics particularly if you have particular preferences or face-related rituals.

One needs a travel-sized grooming pack with toothbrush, shampoo, conditioner, soap, and sunscreen. Remember to pack your preferred names if you value your cosmetics or hair products. Spain may be really hot and dry in the summer; hence it is advisable to pack high SPF sunscreen. You will be outside a lot; hence you should routinely use sunscreen to avoid burns.

Use a heavier lotion for your lips and face if you are heading to northern Spain or during the colder months. Spain's climate is erratic; in winter, particularly in Madrid, where the high altitude causes the air to seem lighter, it may be dry.

Particularly if you use public transit or visit crowded tourist areas, it is a clever idea to pack some travel-sized cleansing wipes and hand sanitizer. Cleaning is highly valued in Spain; hence public restrooms are often maintained spotless. Having these items with you, nevertheless, helps to make travel more leisureful.

Electronics: Maintaining Connection and Charging

Bringing devices when on a trip is essential in the digital age of today for staying connected, finding your route, or leisurely amusement. Although Spain has decent Wi-Fi, it is wise to pack some basic devices to maintain connection and power.

Getting directions, making trip bookings, and staying connected with friends and family all depend on having a fully charged smartphone. Since it allows you to change your devices wherever you go, a power bank comes in really handy. Although Spain's cities provide many charging stations, it is always wise to bring a little power bank for those crucial moments when you most need it.

Bring a camera or a decent phone with adequate capacity to capture images of Spain's stunning landscapes, architecture, and everyday life in photos. Keep additional memory cards or backup batteries in mind if you want to snap many photos.

Finally, be sure you have the correct Spain plug adapters. Spain uses the Type C, E, or F standard European two-pronged plug. Should your gadgets have a different plug, you will require an adapter. If your equipment will not run on Spain's 220V power source, you may want a voltage adaptor.

When preparing for a vacation to Spain, you should be thorough and consider the many activities, climate, and culture you may come across. Wearing the correct clothing, shoes, and accessories will improve your vacation whether your activities include trekking in the Spanish countryside, lounging on Mediterranean beaches, or visiting ancient cities like Madrid and Barcelona. Knowing Spain's climate, packing light and adaptable clothing, and including essential travel gear can help you to completely appreciate the Spanish way of life. Travel great and enjoy your stay in Spain!

CONCLUSION

Spain is a way of life that will permanently affect your soul, not merely a destination to visit. When you consider your trips throughout Spain's sun-kissed landscapes, charming villages, and energetic cities, you bring home not just memories but also deeper understanding of what Spain is all about.

Real travel is about the connections you create, not just about the locations you visit. The echoes of flamenco's passionate pulse, the residual taste of rich Rioja wine, and the friendliness of Spanish hospitality all help to remind you that. Whether it is the delight of sharing a dish of paella, the amazement of seeing the Alhambra at sunset, or the peace of walking along the Camino de Santiago, every experience becomes a treasured component of your holiday.

Spain teaches you to value the simple pleasures in life—like savoring a meal at a slow pace, spending time, and celebrating with friends and total strangers. Deeply ingrained in hundreds of years, its traditions still blossom in the hearts of its people and provide a glimpse into a civilization that values passion, workmanship, and community primarily.

Made in the USA
Columbia, SC
12 July 2025

60650471R00050